for Tom –

THE COSMIC CIRCLE

With blessings
+ good legal
Service!

Edward P Echlin

7. 3 0. 0 7

Oxford

The Cosmic Circle
Jesus and Ecology

Edward P. Echlin

the columba press

First published in 2004 by
the columba press
55A Spruce Avenue, Stillorgan Industrial Park,
Blackrock, Co Dublin

Cover by Bill Bolger
Origination by The Columba Press
Printed in Ireland by ColourBooks Ltd, Dublin

ISBN 1 85607 451 X

Acknowledgements
The author and publisher gratefully acknowledge the permission of the
following to use copyright material: Doubleday & Co Inc for quotations
from *A Marginal Jew, Rethinking the Historical Jesus, Vol 1* by John Meier;
The Liturgical Press for quotations from *The Baptism of Jesus in the
Jordan, the Trinitarian and Cosmic Order of Salvation* by Kilian McDonnell;
Faber and Faber for a quotation from *Thought and Image* by Edwin Muir.
Biblical quotations are from the *Revised Standard Version* and are used
by permission.

Table of Contents

Preface

In the almost startling hymn in his letter to Colossians, Paul of Tarsus, the first Christian writer, exclaims that 'all things' are created and cohere in, through, and for Jesus of Nazareth, 'the image of the invisible God'. For anyone committed to both Jesus Christ and to God's earth, these words rinse and ring through his or her being. Repeatedly, people tell me that their faith in 'the light of the gospel of the glory of Christ' and their love of planet earth coalesce, they go together like sea and land. Now two millennia after Jesus and Paul walked the earth, our earth community declines and deteriorates under relentlessly unsustainable human behaviour, even climate abuse. This book is written for people who care, in the prayerful hope that each of us, especially but by no means only Christians, will look long and prayerfully at Jesus and ecology.

Recently, I have been privileged to speak to inter-religious groups, especially Jews and Christians, and Bahá'í, about our shared faith in our Creator, our mutual concern for the earth and its future, and the distinctive contribution of religion to the earth's flourishing. The religions, as Dermot Lane notes, offer hope. I have learned that every world religion has its distinctive contribution, in a chorus of concern for the earth. I am profoundly aware (not to say afire!) that the Christian contribution is both distinctive and vitally helpful and hopeful.

The cosmos may be imagined as a circle, in which Jesus, God's present, living Word, fills all things. Indeed Jesus' life was a circle filling the cosmos: viewed clockwise at quarter hours, there is birth, Nazareth, public life, death, and completing the circle, resurrection and ascension 'far above all the heavens', as

Paul said, 'filling all things'. We are here to discover Jesus everywhere in his creatures, to let his glory through, as Gerard
Manley Hopkins said Mary did in giving birth to Jesus, to make
the whole earth sacramental. By this I mean we are here to let the
earth radiate, testify to, shine with the pleroma, or fullness, of
the present cosmic Christ. The poet Patrick Kavanagh envisioned magi travelling in three blackthorn bushes huddled into
the December wind on his Monaghan farm. In spring the Holy
Spirit shone through 'yellow flame-blossoms of the whin', and
'seed like stars against the black eternity of April clay'. In brief,
we are here to let the earth shine forth with the glory of God.

The life and death and triumph of Jesus, incarnate within the
earth community, is salvation ecology as well as salvation history.
We impoverish the Christian contribution, and therefore other
religions and the earth, when we restrict God's loving presence
to humans alone. Christians are Christ existing as community.
In him we are plant and animal, soil and water, trees and climate
and stars people. Earth abuse rejects God present in his creatures,
approaches blasphemy, and may be the definitively defiant sin
against the Holy Spirit. This book consists of an introductory
chapter, a chapter on method, 'our way of proceeding', four
chapters on the youth, baptism, ministry, and Jerusalem climax
and triumph of Jesus, with a concluding practical chapter. Some
readers will prefer to read the conclusion first. Unlike the author, it is readers' privilege to commence at the end should they
wish.

I am indebted to more people than I can mention. I am grateful
to Prof C. F. D. Moule for his wise insights, in our shared Sussex
days, into the New Testament. I have incorporated his suggestions in the chapters on Jesus' life and death. I am grateful for
some conversations with Bishop James Jones, of Liverpool, and
his environmental adviser and gardener, Phil Leigh. I also thank
Bishop N. T. Wright, of Durham, for his patient and learned answers to my repeated questions at Westminster Abbey. Fr Dermot
Lane, President of Mater Dei Institute, and parish priest of
Ballaly, Dublin deserves mention for his abiding encouragement

of ecological theology, and his persistent insistence on the cent-
rality of hope, the future, eschatology in Christian theology and
life. Also within these pages are insights received from
Professors Brendan McConvery CSsR, and Con Casey CSsR, at
Marianella, Dublin. I am especially indebted to Dr Geoffrey
Turner, of the University College of Trinity and All Saints,
Leeds, for the privilege of serving as Honorary Research Fellow
in his fine Theology Department. Gratitude is due to Rolf
Killingbeck, Rachel Davis, Mary Grey, and especially Sheila
Milne for reading the manuscript and providing helpful sugges-
tions. I am deeply grateful to Seán O Boyle, for the privilege of
publishing at The Columba Press. I dedicate this book to
Barbara Echlin, upon whom, without flaw, as Chesterton said of
his wife Frances, 'there shines the sign which Guthrum saw'
when he brought peace upon the sea.

Edward P. Echlin
Bexhill, East Sussex
2004

CHAPTER ONE

Introduction: Where on earth I am

In colours of such simple creed
All things sprang at him, sun and weed,
Till the grass grew to be grass indeed
And the tree was a tree at last.
(G. K. Chesterton, *The Ballad of the White Horse*)

I imbibed earth knowledge as a boy, growing up among the translucent trout streams, black and gloomy pine trees, and warm golden sands of Michigan, my native state and boyhood home. Michigan is no longer as fresh and pristine as it was when I grew up in that water wonderland. Winterised second homes, with central heating, line the shores of inland lakes through which I travelled on 'canoe trips', as a boy at summer camp. The speckled and brown trout, the rainbows and graylings still swim in the rivers. But they are fewer, as are the porcupines and black bears along the banks, and the rivers less biodiverse. People need the companionship of the porcupines and the bears, the trout and the rivers, and the whole soil community of creatures, as did the woodland Native Americans, who lived sustainably with Michigan's biodiverse creatures before the *couriers de bois*, the lumberjacks, the settlers, and then the developers arrived. Now that we humans are here, in Michigan and everywhere, in immense numbers and with chainsaws, the earth community needs a *responsible* humanity if earth life is to survive. At present rates of consumption of non-renewable, and even renewable, re-sources, we would need two or three additional planets to accommodate us. We are rapidly quenching earth's biodiverse exuberance. Grizzlies and moose have long disappeared from Michigan. This sober context is where earth spirituality is literally vital. This book centres earth spirituality in Jesus, Lord of the rivers, the animals, and the land. Jesus, the earth, and the church are inseparable. They are symbiotic, they go together like a speckled trout, glinting in the morning sun, and the shining river through which it moves. As the Creator God, incarnate and risen, as God's presence on earth, Jesus is within the earth community, inviting his human creatures to take responsibility for the earth's welfare, and to conduct earth's symphony of praise of God. Earth's welfare is holistic: it includes animals, peace among people, liberation from injustice, and, in brief, sharing earth's gifts, sustainably and especially locally, so that wars, human poverty, earth abuse, and extinction of other creatures are eliminated.

A few years ago, as the second millennium slipped into history, I wrote a book about earth spirituality, which touched more lives than some other books I have written. I write articles, booklets, and books -- this is my sixth book -- because, like most writers, I want some thoughts to 'get around' as only writing does. Sometimes an article or book, like Dutch beer, reaches places other messages don't. How, where, and why a book travels is fascinating, and would stretch the skills of good detectives. In my experience, a book, especially these days, gets to most places on earth. In its wake it invariably brings work, in the form of lectures, seminars, panels, consultations, interviews, correspondence, and eventually demands for another book. I intended *Earth Spirituality: Jesus at the Centre* to be my last book, if not last word. I am writing this one which, with more conviction, I intend to be my last, because so many who read *Earth Spirituality* requested another book.

Fortunately, those of us who are Christians who care about the earth are not alone. Others too care, who live within what Jacques Dupuis SJ, calls 'a superabundant richness and variety of the self-manifestation of God to humanity'. I have worked with some of this 'richness and variety', especially among Jews and Bahá'í. I have learned, and profoundly appreciate, that environmentalists of other religions respond to God's disclosure in different ways, and that they too care about the earth. This book, however, is not directly about inter-religious ecology as such, welcome though such books are. My primary concern is with God's disclosure in Jesus Christ. In subsequent chapters I shall discuss Jesus in his years at Nazareth, and in his period in the Jordan wilderness, in his public ministry, his climactic days at Jerusalem, and as risen Lord of the cosmos. In this introductory chapter, and in a conclusion, I describe some of my own experiences in this new millennium, in which I have been engaged in earth spirituality, theology, and practice.

God is present in the evolution of our cosmos, in the whole evolving earth community, in which we are embedded members, and for which we are responsible. Just as we need reconciliation, so does the whole earth community, which is affected by all that we do, and fail to do. To heal and reconcile people is to heal the earth. The central point of this book is that God so loves the material world, this earth in which we are embedded, that in Jesus he lives in the midst of the earth community. In Jesus God's Word becomes flesh and dwells among us, reconciling the whole creation. As the Archbishop of Canterbury, Rowan Williams, says, 'The heart of the Christmas message is that God takes our material world completely seriously. He doesn't just send a message, he comes to live in the physical world in the flesh and blood of a real person, Jesus.' I hope these pages will speak to Christians, including young people who are uncertain about the Christian way and its relevance to their lives and to ecology. I hope it will interest others walking what Dupuis calls different 'paths' or 'ways'. I also welcome other earth committed people, such as deep ecologists and eco-psychologists I have met, who profess themselves ecological and spiritual, but not religious.

Our New Context
As awareness of earth abuse gradually increases, even among politicians and journalists, so paradoxically does relentless – and avoidable – exploitation. As awareness and exploitation increase, so do demands on the minority of Christians engaged in

earth care. They are a minority, fortunately growing. Recently, when a Catholic bishop said to a lay friend, after a lecture, 'We're all green now', his lay friend corrected him, saying, 'Catholic Christians still have a way to go before we are fully reconciled to the fragility of our earth, and its limits.' But he later observed that, in fact, his bishop friend had moved: although he 'didn't know what he was talking about' when he said all Christians are now 'green', at least he no longer thinks earth concern an aberration, to be feared. With encouragement and nurture he may actually become a green bishop! This uncommon incident illustrates our changing context. The bishop and his friend illustrate the presence of God's Spirit in the whole Christian community, gently inspiring us to accept responsibility for the earth, created and reconciled in Jesus. To recycle a groovy word of the sixties, if we listen to each other in 'co-responsibility' for the earth, we may also hear, and be able to reach, some sensitive young people. We can learn from them, and they from us. In recent words of Bishop James Jones of Liverpool, 'If we wish to engage with a new generation we have got to recognise that Jesus has gone ahead of us, and is already by his Spirit, unknown to them speaking about his concerns for the future of his creation.'

In lecturing and listening to different groups, and to individuals, throughout the British Isles, I am struck at the awakening of many, in almost 'Damascus Road' experiences, to the fragility of the earth, and our responsibility to heal and conserve it. People are also discovering that 'sustainable development' or, better, sustainable sufficiency, is a massive challenge, which demands sacrifice. Creation and redemption go together. The blessing includes the cross, the cross the blessing. In words of a joint statement by the Ecumenical Patriarch of Constantinople and Pope John Paul II:

> A solution at the economic and technological level can be found only if we undergo, in the most radical way, an inner change of heart, which can lead to a change in lifestyle and of unsustainable patterns of consumption and production. A

genuine conversion in Christ will enable us to change the
way we think and act.

Such unavoidable change does not mean gloomily surrendering
what is necessary for happiness. Indeed, in the Christian tradition, sacrifice is joyful. Joyful sacrifice now includes treading
more gently on the earth. It requires a more responsible and re-
spectful attitude to the earth's limits and restraints than has been
prevalent since World War II. In Britain, for example, successive
governments propose patently unsustainable airport expansion
with little responsible opposition from other major parties. An
earth and climate bashing 'freedom to fly' group, demanding
ever more runways, blends exploiting captains of air industry
with politicians from all the major parties. The reason given for
such massive, and irreversible, damage to soil, aquifers, wildlife
habitats, climate, and quality of life is human 'freedom to fly'.
Britain must be 'competitive with Germany and France'. Simon
Jenkins writes:

> The external costs of this mobility are high. We are burning
> up so much fuel, polluting the atmosphere, we are stressed,
> crowded, and no-one's at home. We should be using the tax
> system to encourage people to move less, or at least to bear
> the real costs of movement. But the government is not listen-
> ing. I've never known a government so vulnerable to expen-
> sive lobbying as this one.[1]

Meanwhile, France too expands airports, damaging uniquely
precious garden France, its countryside, biodiversity, and climate. Environmentalists in both countries respond that co-operation, not competition, with less addiction to fossil fuel, is the
only sustainable way forward. A helpful example is a major
French food multiple which claims that, since 2002, 95 per cent
of its merchandise is grown and processed in France. Only 5 per
cent, such as tea, coffee, bananas, and chocolate, is imported.
This is a grand step towards localisation, eliminating unsustainable air freight, that other multiples, and shoppers, hopefully
may follow.

In this challenging context, I suspect I would be fully engaged in earth ministry even were I not an earth theologian. For nothing is more urgent than reversing the destruction of the earth, and rehabilitating the earth community which people have damaged. Earth ministry, from horticulture to conservation to campaigning, including the ministry of ecological theology, must keep adapting to changing environmental contexts. To cite a seismic example, in the late eighties Prime Minister Margaret Thatcher's now famous 'green speech', acknowledging human induced climate change, was a startling context shifting event, like Chernobyl and September 11th, only different. That green speech left even articulate environmentalists muttering 'blimey'. For a prominent world leader to do what Mrs Thatcher had done was a marker in the human relationship with the earth. Politics, at least the way politicians talk, has never been quite the same since.

Nevertheless, even in the rippling wake of that speech it remained difficult to convince Christians, not least those in Mrs Thatcher's 'friends of the car' party, that climate disruption has anything to do with the Christian religion. When, after her speech, I sent a small cheque to my diocesan bishop to support the diocese's earth ministry, my cheque was returned politely with the explanation that the diocese's mission was 'to the spiritual and social needs of people'. Small wonder that the first lady Prime Minister soon disassociated herself from the passion of her own speech, and realigned with the three 'grey' parties (as disempowered Greens call them), and their reckless demands for more 'economic growth'; 'predict and provide' roads, houses, and runways; privatisation of rail, water, and services; 'rationalisation' of family farms; and dependence on imported food and pharmaceuticals. We are still in the wake of that momentous speech. Christian environmentalists, including some diocesan bishops and free church leaders, are increasing, and beginning to offer a significant contribution of earth inclusive justice and peace, concern for animals and biodiversity, responsibility for the earth's future, and sustainable sufficiency; in a word, earth spirituality. The Christian contribution is one of many contributions. It is distinctive because Christians who care about the earth are committed to God present in Jesus, 'the first born of all creation' (Col 1:15), incarnate and risen, Creator and Saviour, who emptied himself into our earth. Through, with, and in him, all creatures in heaven and on earth, and beneath the sea, glorify God in a cosmic alleluia (Phil 2:6-10).

Stewardship or Responsibility?
Since the Renaissance, and especially the scientific awakening of the seventeenth century, Christian thought about the earth has combined 'natural theology', or reasoning to God's presence and might from 'the things that he has made' (Rom 1:20; Wis 13:1-9), with some selective biblical texts. Frequently used texts include the Genesis creation narratives, the perennially popular Noah story, the Psalms and prophets, and some Pauline hymns. It has been argued that people are 'stewards' of the whole earth community. The 'stewardship' model is now deeply ingrained, it is even within our liturgies. While stewardship can be useful and has a biblical resonance, it easily lends itself to a detached, manipulative view of creation, with humans as chief players, and the rest of the earth community 'resources' for human use and enjoyment. With the widely adopted stewardship model, exploitation and dismemberment of the earth has persisted, not least among Christians. Richard Bauckham, of St Andrew's University, says stewardship 'has a biblical and Christian ring to it, which no doubt helps to commend it to us. But it is not a term the Bible itself uses of the human relationship to the rest of creation, nor was it used in this way by the Fathers, the medieval theologians or the Reformers.'[2]

Stewardship has not moved hearts. It has permitted what John Papworth calls 'profit and power people' to justify exploitation, from the Arctic wilderness to the Persian Gulf because, they argue, people are God's stewards. Nor has stewardship moved the hearts of young people. Even with the environment embedded in the curriculum, and included in RE, teenagers show little enthusiasm for taking responsibility for the earth. Recent surveys confirm unsuspected lack of interest in the environment among the 18 to 35 age group. In writing and lecturing, I have questioned the adequacy of the stewardship model.[3] We need models of the human presence, dominion if you wish, drawn from imaginative contemplation of the Bible, the church 'in its teaching, life and worship' and from the earth itself. The earth almost palpably celebrates soft rain, clear rivers, biodiversity, open spaces, woods and wilderness, and the bounteous gifts of harvest. Trees that bear apples are an annual miracle climaxing every autumn. We notice in the Bible that people are God's representatives within all this beauty, his image, here on earth, in a community of creatures. In the Holy Saturday 'Festival of Lights', in the *Exultet* hymn, we consciously praise God with other creatures. When we place a lighted candle in water, we celebrate Christ's reconciliation of the whole cosmos. We rejoice as the explicit voice of all creation's praise, 'Rejoice, heavenly powers! Sing, choirs of angels! Exult, all creation around God's throne!'

A curious phenomenon often occurs after green gatherings, which my wife Barbara calls 'the revivalist syndrome'. That is, at conferences and immediately after lectures and discussions, people voice impressive resolutions. Sustainability takes a small step forward. But then people return home. As after Mrs Thatcher's green speech, or an Earth Summit, nothing much seems to happen – at least nothing like those impressive resolutions. Occasionally, I have asked secretaries of groups, whether they have noticed increased support from regions where recently I had lectured. Sometimes the response is encouraging. More often it is relatively slight, a few enquiries, perhaps a new member or two, but little more. When later I meet people who once resolved vocally to run with the torch, the flame sometimes seems smothered by the socialisation of re-entering a home community. Yet, there is movement, at least beneath the surface. A few intercessions find their way into services, a few more fruit trees are planted, a few more vegetable beds dug and cultivated, sometimes with children participating, more locally produced

food bought, fewer flights booked, more resistance to militarism
and, most significantly, support for Christian environmentalists
not only increasing but what Samantha Chandler of ASWA
(Anglican Society for the Welfare of Animals) calls 'workers' of-
fering their services. People rarely mutate 'once in a flash' like
Paul approaching Damascus, but take small steps, which is better than stunning politicians and media with an electrifying
speech, only to blend back into long grey ranks. Despite the 'revivalist syndrome', more people are realising the connections
between Christianity – and all world religions – and responsibility for the earth.

Walking One's Talk, and Green Breaks
A frequent sticking point for earth spirituality in consumerist
cultures is what liberation theology calls 'practice', what environmentalists call 'walking one's talk'. Alternative economics has
come up with 'best practice', meaning when someone gets it
right make the practice contagious. Francis of Assisi urged his
friars to do the same, praying and studying 'not so much to
know how to speak, but to put into practice what they had
learned and, after having practised it, to propose it to the action
of others'.[4] To persuade people to love and conserve the earth,
environmentalists only 'after having practised it', can 'propose
it to others'. Earth spirituality in the abstract can not only be self-
indulgent, it can stir resentment. Sustainable best practice reaches more people than a lifetime of semi-detached preaching, writing or lecturing. As the last century ended both Mother Teresa
and Pope John XXIII repeated Assisi's lesson: what one is and
does is the best evangelisation. Environmentalists agree.

The demands on time and energies, especially since *Earth
Spirituality* got around, combined with the demands of an organic fruit and vegetable garden, make holidays a rare luxury.
Yet everyone – including Barbara and myself – needs breaks from
'toiling, rejoicing, sorrowing', from what in the Jesuits we called
de more, business as usual. So in lieu of conventional 'full time'
holidays, we sometimes combine meetings, lectures, and confer-

ences in different parts of the UK and Ireland with short breaks, or 'long weekends', in these storied islands. We choose venues hospitable to peke guests. Pekes can be demanding, even imperious. But they are unsurpassed visual aids, a furry demonstration of love and interdependence, part of the family, dependent for life's necessities, such as food, water, and love. A microcosm of how all the world now depends on humans, while humans remain dependent on God the real owner of the earth and its creatures (Is 66:2), pekes, who are lovers of love, are also love's teachers. They remind us that when we withhold love, when we treat other creatures as 'resources', even when we call our exploitation 'rights', or 'free trade', or 'freedom to fly', or 'progress', we starve the poor, other earth creatures and especially ourselves, of life's necessities, of which love is paramount. Perhaps we could assist our children to understand life and love better than we do if we let animals join them more often at school. As Dostoevsky said, 'Children should be pupils with the animals, with the horse, the cow, the dog. Their souls will be better, and they will comprehend more.'

When we first learned, from Professor John Whitelegg, an early specialist in transport, about the damage of air travel, we abandoned annual trips to Andalucia, and experimented with self-catering breaks in the British Isles. But again we learned, from environmentalists, and from John Gummer MP, when he was environment minister in the nineties, that swelling population, migration, and above all family splintering mean that 'second homes', even if used at times for self-catering, add to housing shortages, with concomitant pressure for more housing on shrinking green fields, including starter homes in villages such as those in which we self-catered. So we now share roofs, boilers, power, and grounds in guest houses and hotels. Which is not to suggest that these always become sustainable 'best practice'. They reduce pressure for new houses. But many, with superfluous packaging, laundry, imported food and drink, including distant wine with plastic 'corks', and even climate damaging air conditioning, are themselves unsustainable.

Nevertheless, as 'customers' we are 'always right', we get our chance to write comments at the end of visits. We need more imaginative eco-caterers, who provide regional food and drink, with insulation and renewable energy, and support local growers of organic food and happy animals. Eco-catering is a growing opportunity for family business. Despite the privatised disarray in which the last Tory government left railways and buses, whenever possible we travel by train. Even in privatised Britain, trains and buses remain, save only foot and pedal, the most sustainable form of transport. Shared transport is relatively fast and safe, and a less stressful way to travel, permitting travellers to read, write, view the countryside, and even dine while moving, which is something no car travel can match.

Thrice yearly, in awakening March, after potatoes are sown, and migrant birds are on the wing, and in apple ripe September, we enjoy week breaks, often in Celtic Wales or Ireland, or on the continent. Like neighbours and fellow parishioners, living near the south coast, we can easily reach other parts of our heritage, just across the English Channel. The one downside to northern continental visits is that, without vaccination, we cannot take Bertha with us. Vaccination, with inserted chips or weeks caged in quarantine, is for a humanoid peke unthinkable. Pekes, like other pets, are another reason for homeland holidays. When we do go to the continent, we have a friend live in here with Bertha, or take her for a break of her own in a peke friendly home. Both ways she gets prime treatment, even spoiling, but we miss her company. And she makes us feel bad when, as suitcases appear, she retreats disconsolately to her bed.

In May or September, or sometimes in June when the garden is planted and occupied, we have travelled by train to the Low Countries, Germany, and France. If a country's wealth is ultimately in its soil, its aquifers, and climate, and transmitted rural wisdom, then garden France is undoubtedly one of the richest biosystems on earth. But soil is also fragile. France's precious soil now suffers from expanding airports, roads, second homes, agribusiness, and internal migration of young country people,

detached custodians of centuries of rural wisdom, to car clut-
tered cities. Peasant wisdom, and traditions, still linger in
France, but the soil and cuisine lore is dwindling, to the loss of
the whole world. Possibly France which, paradoxically, is not
known for its animal welfare, should follow Dostoevsky's advice, and introduce animals to classrooms. France, like most
other countries, developed and developing, seems to have lis-
tened too uncritically to modern economists, of whom
Kirkpatrick Sale writes:

> Economists are taught to measure the value of 100 bushels of
> wheat coming off a farm, but have no way of factoring in the
> topsoil eroded or poisoned in the process, the damage to the
> surrounding ecosystem, the effect of toxic run-off from fer-
> tilisers in streams and bays, or the enormous environmental
> costs of mass producing artificial fertilisers, pesticides, and
> high-tech farm machinery. Economists ignore this informa-
> tion not because they are idiotic, cruel or dumb, but because
> they are conditioned by their training to see the natural
> world only as resources; they do not understand the com-
> plexities of the science of ecology.[5]

We enjoyed a fleeting March week at Chartres, above the Ile de
France and the Beauce, 'the golden granary of Paris', visiting
twice daily in gradually lengthening light the cathedral's teaching in glass and stone. The glass, especially the blue pierced with
light, the stone, the cathedral itself, rising like a prayer on its
ridge, are a visual gospel. The whole of salvation history, and
salvation ecology too, unfold in Chartres, beginning with the
oldest Genesis creation story. In the north aisle, the famous
Noah window portrays the rainbow covenant between God and
people and animals. The Jesus history includes the animals at
the manger, the Nazareth years, Jesus' parables and ministry,
the cosmic cross, and Jesus risen, king of the universe. When in
France, we attend Mass on Sundays and, when possible, during
the week. Cathedral communities are usually larger than villages, probably because there are resident priests, and the worshippers, who include visitors like ourselves, come from a larger,
more populous catchment.

After Chartres, we visited in bright June Laon, the hilltop cathedral town, or 'crowned mountain' where, as at Chartres, a great medieval theology 'school' of masters and students flourished for a time. John Scotus Eriugena, a Celtic light of darker ages, lived and studied there, centuries before the Laon medieval school. Anselm and Ralph of Laon, the outstanding medieval scholars there, made Eriugena's writings widely known. Another luminary, Peter Abelard, briefly studied there under Anselm, raising questions that would be debated for centuries. Apart from memories of the school, Laon is especially memorable for its hilltopper oxen on the cathedral towers, a touching tribute by medieval masons to these sturdy companions, who dragged large stones to the hilltop, as no horse could do. There the masons fashioned the oxen's burdens into a cathedral crowning the hill. American visitors, especially from the Midwest, appreciate Laon as the birthplace of Jacques Marquette, who may have been baptised in the cathedral, and certainly, as a boy, wondered at its hilltopper oxen, outlined against the sky. As Père Marquette SJ, with Louis Jolliet, Marquette was among the first – perhaps *the* first – Caucasian to view the Mississippi. Marquette noted along the banks of 'old man river', wild buffalo grazing free on the prairies, similar to the hilltopper oxen above Laon. His descriptions of these animals, preserved in *Jesuit Relations*, is perhaps the first time those animals entered written history. It would not be the last! Marquette died, on a canoe voyage of discovery and evangelisation, on Lac Illinois (now Lake Michigan). *Consummatus in breve*, trusted by the Indians, whose language he could speak, Marquette was only thirty-eight years old. Jacques Marquette still has collateral descendants in Laon, named Barbière. He himself lives on in a memorial park, and Rue Père Marquette, in Laon; and, in the New World, in towns, buildings, a railway, a great university, and even a lecture series, in the Great Lakes bioregion where he was based. Marquette did not live to see what the lumberjacks, the settlers, and their growth obsessed successors would do to Illinois culture, to the free-range buffalo, to the lakes, and to the Mississippi. As Robert

Frost, a twentieth-century New England poet, remarked pithily, 'It doesn't take long to destroy a continent.'

We also visited Paris in March. Paris, which enjoyed space for expansion which the hilltop cathedral schools lacked, succeeded Chartres and Laon as the premier medieval school. It held its pre-eminence, eventually becoming a great university and cultural city. Despite subsequent wars and revolutions, industrialisation, cars, suburbs, and tourists, Paris still exudes culture. A visitor barely touches the surface of Paris, its museums, churches, townscape, history, river walks, and restaurants, in a week, or even in many months – but to sojourn in Paris, even for a week in spring is, as Ernest Hemingway said, a moveable feast, something you always take with you. To walk around Notre Dame before breakfast is to experience a 'built environment' about as fine as our species has fashioned. To attend Mass at Notre Dame, with Parisians, and other visitors, is a privilege. The numerous exhibitions – and resident masterpieces – in Paris museums each deserve hours of study. The townscape, river walks, trees, parks, and boulevards help to make Paris liveable. Even now some restaurants still struggle to promote regional meals, with regional recipes, produce, and wines, prepared and presented with Gallic finesse.

Another stunning cathedral we visited is St John the Baptist at Amiens, on the sombre but still fertile Somme. The cathedral honours its patron, and the baptism of Jesus, with splendid carvings of Jesus, with John and his followers, as northern European carvers envisioned those wilderness scenes. Jesus' baptism is important to salvation ecology, with our imminent water crisis, because Jesus sanctified the waters by his presence as our ancient liturgies still testify. Amiens majestically commemorates and symbolically perpetuates that ecological event, which is the topic of chapter four of this book. Unlike Chartres and Paris, Amiens old town was devastated in the last world war. The bombers spared the cathedral itself, but the leaded glass, dissolved in the inferno of a burning city, was totally destroyed.

Another sobering cathedral town, and testimonial to medieval – and Renaissance and baroque – architecture, is Avignon in Provence, the fourteenth-century residence of seven popes. Avignon must be visited in cooler months, of shorter days, for it has become a tourist and performing arts centre. The medieval streets, and the remnants of church buildings and religious communities, are a sombre reminder of where the church went wrong in some ways, and of the anarchical violence of which people are capable. When we forget we are a servant church, we and our leaders the Servant Christ existing as community today, inevitably the world finds us unappealing, even unpleasant. To recall St Francis – and Mother Teresa and John XXIII – again, our servant lives are our first evangelisation.

Green Breaks and White Monks
So much of our better agriculture, our food, farm animals, forestry, wines, and, in general, 'soil community' wisdom derives from the early Cistercians, that a visit to their remains is something of a green pilgrimage. The medieval Cistercians, remote though their houses were, left traces in some cathedral cities, including the remains of their first college at Paris, and another, St John's at Oxford. The early Cistercian lifestyle was what our time would call sustainable: prayer, study, manual work, manuscript preservation, experiments with food and drink, stock rearing, and work in the gardens, fields, orchards, vineyards, rivers and woodland, all near the home abbey, or at nearby granges. To work is to pray, *Labore est orare*, is a Cistercian adage forever relevant when that work is ecologically sustainable and glorifies God. Animal breeds and lore, notably sheep and cattle, are Cistercian legacies, as are forestry techniques, aquaculture, fruit growing and selection, northern irrigation, mill races, and viniculture. Wines we take for granted, including Chardonay, Cabernet Sauvignon, Chablis, Mersault and Ruislip, with cider blending, are Cistercian contributions to the joy and warmth of the human heart. So is the 'greenhouse' which prolongs the growing season in northern climes. There is perennial wisdom that needs recovery in the Cistercian balance

of prayer, study, and manual work, and in their adage that to work is to pray, especially when that work is with the soil. The Orthodox theologian, Vigen Guroian, gardens holistically, like a Cistercian, with prayer, tripods, and vegetables:

Peter, when he saw Jesus in the company of Moses and Elijah, had wanted to build three tabernacles to contain the light. In my dark spring, without even knowing it, I had fulfilled Peter's wish. In August the naked tripods I had built in the pascal season were transformed into translucent tents of woven green life, suffused with resplendent dappled light – timeless, uncontained, and superabundant. Now I stood amidst them in the garden bathed in the light of the sun and filled with the Spirit of God. And with Peter I uttered, 'Lord, it is good for me to be here!'[6]

We began to retrace White Monk footsteps where it all began in 1098, at Citeaux itself, where the mighty movement gathered, where Robert of Molesmes and a handful of followers, including Stephen Harding, settled in the dark forest of Citeaux, in Burgundy. After nearly a thousand years of prayer, work, decline, and dissolution, Citeaux was refounded on that same hallowed spot, by modern Cistercians in 1898. The fertile topsoil, hedges, remnant orchards, vineyards, rivers, woods, and outlying granges, which the white monks and the lay brothers tended, are lovingly cultivated again, a Cistercian legacy to the whole world. When the fertility of well loved soil is cherished, the wise French dictum is very true, *plus ça change, plus c'est la même chose*. Irish farmer and poet, Patrick Kavanagh, who found infinity in small things, expresses the same truth; there is 'undying difference in the corner of a field'. After Citeaux, we visited its 'four oldest daughters': La Ferte, whose guest house remains; beautiful Pontigny, in Chablis vineyard territory, with its photogenic chapel, still in use, its mills, fields, and vineyards; Morimond, including its pews, screen, and pulpit, now safe in Langres Cathedral; and finally Clairvaux, where, in 1115, Citeaux sent a young Bernard of Fontaine to found a fourth daughter in the valley of the Aube, which Bernard characteristi-

cally called Clairvaux, a name which was to be forever linked
with his own. Bernard of Clairvaux became one of the towering
figures, perhaps *the* towering figure, of the twelfth century. His
influence, and the gale of his eloquence, continues still. Sixty-
five daughter abbeys, including Rievaulx and Fountains, are descendants of Clairvaux, a testimony to the magnetism of
Bernard. On a farm in Nidderdale, formerly a grange of
Fountains Abbey, an ancient cooking apple clings to life, which,
according to a local antiquarian who was born there, is a descendant of a tree planted by medieval lay brothers of Fountains.
Citeaux, through the magnetic reach of Bernard of Clairvaux,
has left traces even in the English apple.

Cluny and Bulwick
The Cistercians had an older sibling, a Burgundian rival which
we also visited, founded in southern Burgundy in 909, with a different interpretation of St Benedict's rule. Cluny dominated
western Christendom in the tenth and eleventh centuries, and
rivalled Citeaux in the twelfth. In its medieval prime, with many
benefactors, a splendid, towering basilica, long hours in choir,
and five successive charismatic abbots, Cluny founded and
ruled many, finally too many, daughter priories, of which St
Pancras, in Lewes, was Britain's first and finest. Cluny, like the
St Pancras ruins today, is sobering. Standing at the west entrance of the once dominant church, one looks down upon a car
park. Like Shelly's pyramid of Ozymandias, 'nothing beside remains', save a few stones, and foundations, some towers, and almost audible presences of monks chanting psalms for departed
benefactors, under the fatherly care of Abbots Odo, Odilo,
Mayeul, Hugh, and Peter the Venerable. In the south transept
ruins, a plaque commemorates Peter, who was a local man, as
'one of the purest spirits of the Benedictine order'. It sometimes
befalls pure and great men to preside over the decline of once
proud and useful movements. Peter the Venerable was one of
these men.

That touching plaque to Peter the Venerable curiously recalls

Mervyn Wilson's organic fruit and vegetable garden at his Georgian rectory, in Bulwick, Northamptonshire. In Britain, not only empires decline, so do irreplaceable Georgian and Victorian rectories and gardens. On two trips to nearby Oundle, once to speak to Peterborough clergy on a post-ordination course, and again to preach at Oundle School harvest, we were able, in late autumn, to combine these October lectures with a visit to Mervyn's garden. At that season many of the vegetables, and the early fruit, are already harvested, their remnants rapidly becoming humus on the compost heap, but Mervyn's later apple varieties are literally falling from the trees. On our second visit, we took with us some bags for windfalls, and back home distributed to bemused, and grateful, neighbours Annie Elizabeth, Pitmaston Pineapple, White Magnum Bonum, Adam Pearmain, and a plethora of late keepers, and cookers, of which few had heard. Even in this fertile corner, the lush south-east, local shops stock mainly six boring, chemical saturated, even imported, varieties, their glossy uniformity betraying numerous toxic sprays, perhaps as many as sixteen in a season, sometimes followed by artificially ventilated storage, and air and lorry transport. According to DEFRA, around 150,000 apple acres have been uprooted since 1960. Lush, fruit friendly Devon alone has lost 95 per cent of its orchards.[7]

Living Sustainably Locally

The key to personal sustainability, to healing, restoring, and conserving the earth, letting God's glory through in preparation for God's kingdom, is earth spirituality locally. Local sustainability challenges. Reigning corporate chieftains, their politicians, and trivialising media would have us think, and live, in too globalised a manner. Living, purchasing, gardening, holidaying, and consuming locally, by which I mean, at least, bioregionally, is possible, healthy, sustainable, and even exciting. Living sustainably locally is anything but selfish. Far from depriving developing peoples, our local living helps others conserve, appreciate, and improve their own bioregional fertility, instead of industrialising their local soil for cash crops – degrading their soil fertility and 'virtual water' (to export avocados is to export water) – in exchange for dependence on consumer things and American grain. Lester Brown writes of the peril of dependence on grain imports, 'The risk for the low-income, grain-importing countries is that grain prices could rise dramatically, impoverishing more people in a shorter period of time than any event in history.'[8] Closely related are the two fatal fallacies in globalised 'trade': 1) that fragile soil can be intensively industrialised for export crops (and virtual water) indefinitely; and 2) that there will always be abundant food to import for fossil fuel dependent peoples. Several times, for example, in Israel I said to Israelis working on the land, 'You're destroying your soil.' The reply, echoing the current wisdom was invariably the same, 'That's alright. We can put a factory here for exportable things, and import American food.' Living and exchanging locally, in developed and developing worlds, secures the climate, and the future, not least the future of our children. Unrestricted, or 'neoliberal', trade means more food miles, with immense damage to biosystems and climate, and the whole fragile global environment. Edward Goldsmith notes, 'The real cause of the pervasive environmental destruction is economic development, and unfettered trade which seeks to maximise development, and to which all considerations today, however important, are ruthlessly subordinated.'

For living sustainably locally, a useful rule of thumb is Christian Ecology Link's 'LOAF' principles: Locally produced, Organically grown, Animal friendly, Fairly traded. Some trade is necessary, sustainable, and fair. Northern Europe, for example, depends on other climates, in different ecosystems, for cotton, olives, bananas, citrus, tea, coffee, and cocoa. The 'locally produced' in the LOAF principles does not mean total exclusion of trade, but to import necessities from as close to home as possible, thereby reducing transport, especially climate damaging air freight. A translucent example is the mega gift of wine: 'A day without wine is like a day without sunshine' says the venerable adage, surely not coined in medieval Scandinavia. 'Unfettered trade' in wine and beer can be environmentally damaging, foolish, and unnecessary. In Britain, for example, on the edge of the glorious vineyards of the continent, once Roman vineyards are again green, fragrant, and healthy with vines. In Kent and Sussex, and even in Staffordshire, fine white, sparkling, rosé, and even some red wines delight local connoisseurs, surprise visitors, and are beginning to rival continental wines. Good red – and white – wines from France, Spain, Portugal, and Italy are available from just across the Channel. English wines are available at several large chains, at vineyards, and in local and farm shops, and farmers' markets, which also sell local cider, perry, honey, preserves, and meat. When pubs and hotels and restaurants offer few or no English, or bioregional, wines, it sends a message to order a regional beer or cider – and say why! Principal family shoppers realise that purchasing locally, and sustainably, takes time; it means reading labels, asking questions, shopping around, adapting menus, and sometimes paying more. But the time, effort, and expense assist local businesses, reduce ruinous food miles, lead to surprising discoveries, and encourage distant people to live locally and sustainably too, and contribute to local, and global, sustainable sufficiency.

Our Local Homes
Local sustainability obviously includes the homes where we live. The different ways – and means – people use to lighten their burden on the earth, sometimes even to restore their local habitat, are fascinating. We can make our homes sustainable, whether we live, like Mervyn Wilson, in a Georgian rectory, or alone, or in community, in a house, flat, bungalow, or rest home. I conclude this introduction with the recommendation that we bless our homes – with three adaptations of traditional house blessings. First, let our blessings include not just people and 'built' environment, but garden, plants, and local wildlife, including the companions living in window boxes, and bird feeders. Second, let our blessings be not just once-only events but a

repeated 'best practice', perhaps at winter and summer solstice, when we are especially aware of our 'Brother sun' who symbolises Jesus, 'the Sun out of heaven', as Bishop Melito of Sardis described Our Lord. Third, unless we can borrow a neighbour reader, or deacon, or the like, I suggest that we ourselves bless our homes using a prayer book, or our own composition. We bless our home and garden at both solstices, with our peke on my lap, using a timeworn, somewhat dated, *Priest's New Ritual*, from the last millennium. There is scope for creativity. Hopefully when people discover, or compose, a blessing they like, they will share it through a parish newsletter. Our own homes, even if just a room with window boxes, with their plants and wildlife, are the unique, very special micro-biosystem of this planet for which we are uniquely responsible. How we fulfil that responsibility affects the whole earth, everywhere and forever. Every home is a centre of outward ripples. We can leave our domestic biosystems better than we found them.

Notes:
1. Simon Jenkins, 'Predict and Provide ...?', *Countryside Voice* (Autumn 2002), p. 42.
2. Richard Bauckham, 'Stewardship and Relationship', in *Caring for Creation*, R. J. Berry, ed. (Leicester: Inter-Varsity Press, 2000), p. 99.
3. Edward P. Echlin, *Earth Spirituality, Jesus at the Centre* (New Alresford: Arthur James, 1999/2002), pp. 25-27; cf. also Bill McKibben, *The Comforting Whirlwind: God, Job and the Scale of Creation* (Grand Rapids: Eerdmans, 1994), pp. 51-53.
4. In Mario Masini, *Lectio Divina* (New York: Alba House, 1998), p. 69.
5. Kirkpatrick Sale, 'The Heart of the Matter', *Fourth World Review*, 121 and 122 (2003) p. 12.
6. Vigen Guroian, *Inheriting Paradise, Meditations on Gardening* (London: Darton, Longman & Todd, 2001), p. 53.
7. Sally Twiss, *Apples: A Social History* (London: National Trust, 1999) p. 6.
8. Lester Brown, *Eco-Economy: Building an Economy for the Earth* (London: Earthscan, 2001), p. 167.

CHAPTER TWO

Our Way of Proceeding

The workers of the Society should have
only one foot touching earth,
the other raised to begin a journey.
(Ignatius Loyola)

As an admirer and struggling disciple of Jesus Christ, how can I include the earth in my spirituality, and in my whole lifestyle? To borrow a key phrase from the Jesuit constitutions, what is 'our way of proceeding' in relating discipleship of Jesus with our love of the earth? The shorthand 'our way of proceeding' refers to our game plan and practice, the way we adapt to changing situations, challenges, contexts. Our present situation is grimly, almost dark-humorously, paradoxical. For 1) we live when people are aware that humanity, with ever increasing numbers and technology, is destroying the climate and quenching the biodiversity of the earth, upon which life depends. We are, it has been said, by Sara Parkin and others, the first species ever to monitor minutely our own extinction. We know precisely what we are doing. We can even monitor fossil fuel driven climate change charted on televisions. We know how we could reverse the destruction, live sustainably, and heal, regenerate, and conserve the earth; and yet, 2) we plunge ahead building more roads and runways, building on and intensifying precious agricultural land, modifying (or mutilating!) plant and animal genes, and supporting socially, environmentally, and economically destructive oil wars in the Middle East. I would like briefly to explore our way of proceeding in this lethally paradoxical context. How do we bring the all-inclusive incarnation and reconciliation of Jesus Christ to the suffering earth community? It's a long way from the head to the heart, and from the heart to the hand. Like the first companions of Ignatius Loyola, who coined the phrase 'our way of proceeding', we who care about the earth are like missionaries with 'only one foot touching the earth, the other raised to begin a journey'.

Other Ways

It's usually helpful to mention other ways of proceeding that, while more or less parallel to our own hopes and dreams, are not the road we walk. One is an adapted 'scientific' way, which applies modern scientific and business expertise to God's self-disclosure. This way, echoing the Enlightenment celebration of human reason and powers, appeals to Christians of a scientific or business background, eager to relate empirical methods to God's revelation as narrated in the Bible. Mark Allen Powell, a Lutheran biblical scholar, notes how the Enlightenment eventually influenced religion:

> The enlightenment emphasised the orderliness of nature and so encouraged disciplined scholarship that adheres to well-defined methods of testing and verifying hypotheses. It furthered the organisation of knowledge and the development of critical thinking. Though initially a philosophical movement (featuring such luminaries as Descartes, Locke, Rousseau, and Voltaire), the new orientation led to tremendous advances in science and mathematics. Eventually, its effects were felt on politics and religion.[1]

The difficulty with the Enlightenment influence, and the scientific and business way of proceeding, is that the Bible, within the whole living tradition of the church, infers, echoes, and connotes more than is explicitly verbalised. To borrow Gregory the Great's metaphor, God's disclosure is like a forest. The divine word grows along with those who read it. There is life on the forest floor that an appreciative naturalist discovers more readily than a reductionist botanist. The hymns, literary forms, liturgies, and creeds of the Bible, and the living tradition, do not readily lend themselves to empirical and business methods. The late Dean of Ripon, an accomplished poet, Edwin Le Grice, observed, 'It is important to remember that the language of religion – of scripture and creeds and liturgy – is poetry rather than prose: it conveys more than it states.'[2] Augustine called God a Poet. William Blake noticed that 'the whole Bible is filled with imagination and visions'. Stevie Smith called 'the airy Christ' a 'sweet singer' of songs. The Lakota Sioux, in their devotional art, picture Jesus as the Sun Dancer Christ. When those who regard revelation, 'the two books', with empirical, scientific, and business methods engage with those who contemplate God's word as poetry, and salvation history as facts plus interpretation, there is sometimes difficulty in finding a shared community of discourse.

A somewhat similar approach contents itself with a few familiar scripture texts, enhanced by some high spots and saints in Christian history, and builds a creation spirituality upon them. Scripture texts usually include the Genesis narrative, the Noah story, some Psalms, a few prophetic texts, and some Wisdom texts. From church history, favourites include the Celtic Church, St Benedict, St Francis of Assisi, and Hildegarde of Bingen. This way of proceeding can lead to genuine commitment to God's earth, created and redeemed in Christ. But scripture, as Henri de Lubac said, is not a quarry but a treasure. It glows between the lines, and in the small print. Jesus is God's Word concentrated. The whole scriptures are fulfilled, unified, illuminated, and transcended in him. There are many tributaries in the Christian reality, flowing into a stream both broad and deep, from which we can draw living water for the changing situations in which we live. There are texts that merit special attention, but they are not the whole Christian green heritage. That heritage is within the whole living memory of Jesus, within the Jesus movement, which includes the insights of artists and poets, theologians, parents, religious women and men, and Christian environmentalists.

A third, quite different, way of proceeding which I encounter, while it includes baptised people, distances itself from the church, and even the word 'God'. Some Christians who care deeply about the earth understandably are disenchanted with the earth illiteracy and indifference of churchmen and women. An instance that disturbed, and still challenges, me occurred at an Irish environmentalists' meeting. A cradle Catholic, mother of several children, and concerned about the 'Celtic Tiger's' ravishment of Ireland's earth, atmosphere, and water, said she wanted the present church 'destroyed', so that we could 'rebuild from the rubble'. There are variations on this theme, in Britain as in Ireland, some syncretistic, polytheistic, even pantheistic. Others just want to restore an idealised 'Celtic Church', or something similar. I sincerely sympathise with fellow, and former, Christians, who passionately care about the earth and desire to heal the earth community, but find insufficient encouragement or even interest in church leaders. Yet I think they are misguided in feeling they must look elsewhere, instead of drinking more deeply at the deep wells, and listening to what the Poet God is singing. They would rediscover, as Vatican II did, the baptismal responsibilities of the whole Christian people. Like Peanuts, they would meet the church, and find it is us. *Abusum non tollit usum:* that is, abuse of a good thing is no reason to forsake it. Some people abuse 'the dark stuff', good cool Guinness, which is no reason to forsake 'Arthur'. When a dysfunctional clerical culture, more interested in the gender and sexual orientation of clergy than earth abuse, is not even supportive of communicants who do care about the earth, that culture is dead wrong. Some would say just plain dead. But the sensible response is not to abandon Jesus Christ! Rather take a closer look, listen harder, reconsider 'the breadth and length and height and depth' of God's love poured out for us, and all creation, in Jerusalem (Eph 3:18). Just think about the mind-blowing reality, expressed by Pope Leo I, which is really an aphorism of our own meditation on the gospel: 'He through whom the world was created was brought forth in the midst of creation.' Jesus, God's Word, is immanent, in the earth, inviting our response. Jesus deserves the loyalty of Christian environmentalists, now more than ever.

One other way, which may be described as the inter-religious way, brings world religions together, just as ecumenical ecology brings ecclesial communities and churches together. A few examples of this beautifully hopeful rapprochement are the meetings of religions at Assisi and Nepal; inter-religious cruises; joint efforts of Muslims, Jews and Christians in the Society for the Protection of Nature in Israel; co-operation between Christian Ecology Link and the Jewish sponsored Noah Project; and the presentation, before the Queen and Prince Philip, of their creation faith in Whitehall Banqueting Hall, by eleven world religions. I attended that presentation, and was moved by Prince Philip's keynote remarks, the presentations, and the concluding words of the Ecumenical Patriarch Bartholomew. It is gratifying to co-operate with other religions which, in their distinctive ways, respond ecologically to 'tremendous and fascinating mystery' in the earth, to what Pope John Paul II calls 'the common, fundamental element and the common root'. Muslims include the earth in submission to Allah, and the mediation of the prophet Mohammed. Hindus respect creation and engage with the oneness of Brahma-Atman. Buddhists find peace in Nirvana. Jews include the integrity of creation in their work for justice and peace. The inter-religious way increases the religious contribution to care for the earth. As Patriarch Bartholomew remarked:

> Not to respect the creation, but to destroy it, is a sin. It transcends all social problems. Religions share this view; Muslims, Roman Catholics, Jews, Protestants ... whatever our theological differences, we agree on this. If we give bread to the poor but it is contaminated bread, we are not helping them. If we destroy everything today, then how will our children and our grandchildren survive?[3]

Our Way

Our distinctive Christian 'way of proceeding', as we respond to the cry of creation, is, in brief, to take 'a long loving look at the real' Christian reality, seeking discoveries in Jesus, and in 'the teaching, life, and worship' of the church, and putting these discoveries *into practice*. Within the Christian reality, I include the still living memory of Jesus that preceded the New Testament, the whole Bible, and the continuing, living Christian tradition. In words of the Catholic Council Vatican II, 'The Church, in her teaching, life, and worship, perpetuates and hands on to all generations, all that she herself is, all that she believes' (*Divinum Verbum*, 8). With wonder, we also discover 'signals of transcendence', reality as created, in 'the second book', in the created, evolving cosmos itself. As Tertullian said in the second century, 'God is first known from nature; and afterwards authenticated by instruction: from nature by his works; by instruction through his revealed announcements' (*Against Marcion*, 1, 18). We proceed with wonder, described by Emily Dickinson as 'a beautiful, but bleak condition, he has not lived who has not felt'. Ignatius Loyola adds a gripping, imaginative twist to wonder, when he suggests we should be filled with wonder, that other creatures support, and do not destroy us, despite our sin. His words are especially compelling now, as we extinguish fellow creatures and whole habitats almost daily. As temperatures rise, and floods increase, we may also 'wonder' how long our fellow creatures will tolerate our abuse:

> The fifth point is an exclamation of wonder, with intense affection, running through all creatures in my mind, how they have suffered me to live, and have preserved me in life; how the angels, who are the sword of the Divine Justice, have borne with me, and have guarded and prayed for me; how the saints have been interceding and praying for me; and the heavens, the sun, the moon, the stars, and the elements, the fruits of the earth, the birds, the fishes, and the animals; and the earth, how it is it has not opened to swallow me up, creating new hells that I might suffer in them for ever.[4]

We just noted that oral memories of Jesus preceded the writing of the New Testament. Mark Allen Powell notes that very early hymns celebrated God's actions in Jesus. Some, which included the cosmos, were later incorporated in the New Testament:

> Before the gospels, before the epistles, before Josephus, even Q, people were writing hymns about Jesus. A few of them even get quoted in the Bible. The hymns were there before

anyone tried to write a narrative of Jesus' life or reflect systematically about his identify and message. They were inspired by a story that was beginning to emerge, a story that defied simple chronological distinction between past and present, then and now.[5] Orthodox theologian, John Anthony McGuckin, observes that still older hymns, from other religions, preceded Christian hymns, and influenced Christian preaching and liturgies. 'Some fine poetic examples still exist, not least the 'Hymn to Amen Ra' from Egypt, and the Stoic 'Hymn to Zeus' by Cleanthes, or the 'Hymn to Apollo at the feast of Karna.'[6] Through their influence on our hymns, these other hymns indirectly influenced our Bible and our worship. Those milestone events in our worship, which we call rites of passage, or sacraments, which draw indirectly from pre-Christian hymns, help us prepare for God's kingdom, they inaugurate the new creation. Jean Danielou SJ writes, 'The sacraments were thought of as the essential events of Christian existence ... In them was inaugurated a new creation which introduced the Christian even now into the kingdom of God.'[7] Our final goal is the worship of Jesus with all creation. A liturgical scholar, Francis Mannion, writes, 'Salvation embraces not only the individual person, but all that God has made. In its cosmic dimension, the liturgy gathers up every feature of creation into itself.'[8] And Leonardo Boff, an early liberation theologian, says of the inclusion of all creatures in our praise of God, we are 'in communion with all earthly things, to share in a universal brotherhood and a cosmic democracy. Human praise joins the seminal praise that all things, without interruption, give to the Creator. Man, at long last reconciled, celebrates the world as a paradise, because he himself has gone through a fundamental change.'[9]

That Beautiful Power
To make discoveries in our whole Christian reality, in our 'teaching, life, and worship', in all that we are and believe, and to relate our discoveries to our lives, we need imagination. As

Karl Barth said, 'A man without imagination is more an invalid than a man without a leg.' Lack of imagination, combined with a huge deficit in sustainable practice, is the principal reason for the widely, and correctly, perceived ecological inadequacies of the church. Imagination is difficult to define. Samuel Taylor Coleridge, however, describes our imaginative power beautifully – and with imagination!

> This light, this glory, this fair luminous mist,
> This beautiful, and beauty-making power …
> All melodies the echoes of that voice,
> All colours a suffusion from that light.
> *(Dejection: An Ode)*

Imagination mobilises sense experience, intuitive perception, and memory. It adds colour, light, tone, shape, depth, touch, and melody to our thoughts. We cannot grasp the earth-inclusive beauty of God's saving self-disclosure with conclusions from abstract premises. As William Temple observed, there are no abstract revealed truths, only truths of revelation. Ignatius Loyola directs us to see, with the eyes of the imagination, God's self-disclosure, in Nazareth of Galilee: 'Seeing the spot: here it will be to see the whole space and circuit of the terrestrial globe, in which so many divers races dwell: then likewise behold in particular the house and chamber of our Lady in the town of Nazareth in the province of Galilee.'[10] With imagination we see Jesus within the soil community of Nazareth, and with the water, and water creatures, of the Jordan, in the wilderness, and at the sea, fields, hills, and valleys, and with the domestic animals and wildlife of Galilee. Imaginatively we see Jesus in his ministry, in the villages and fields, and at the Lake, and in Judea, in Jerusalem, and on the cosmic cross which embraces the whole cosmos, all that is created, visible and invisible. With imagination we also hear Jesus' words, in solidarity with millions who have heard his words in the scriptures, in preaching, and in the *Spiritual Exercises*. In the *Ave Verbum*, the *Panis Angelicus*, the *Salve Regina*, and Schubert's *Ave Maria*, we almost hear, we intimate, the inexhaustible depths of the meaning of the incarnation.

With Augustine, William Blake, and Stevie Smith, we listen, with the ears of our imagination, to Jesus, the Son of God, coming to us as Poet, and Singer of Songs. With theological poets, artists, musicians, and environmentalists, we can listen anew with the ears of the imagination to the beautiful songs, about heaven and earth, that the Poet God is singing. Walt Whitman writes:

After the seas are all crossed,
After the great Captains have accomplished their work,
After the noble inventor, finally shall come the Poet worthy the name,
The true Son of God shall come singing his songs.

We see, listen, and respond, with our whole persons, to Jesus, and our living Christian reality, when it touches our hearts. John Henry Newman took as his motto: *Cor ad cor loquitur*, heart speaks to heart. Newman said, 'Man is not a reasoning animal; he is a seeing, feeling, contemplating, acting animal.' The heart, he said, 'is commonly reached, not through the reason, but through the imagination, by means of direct impressions, by the testimony of facts and events, by history, by description. Persons influence us, voices melt us, looks subdue us, deeds inflame us.'[11] It is the whole person, in her or his totality, that sees, listens, connects, and reasons. It is the whole concrete, earth embedded being that comprehends. As Newman said, 'The whole man moves.'

Our Words

Our community *words* too enlighten us. Even in a globalised media age, we remain great talkers. A day without words is like a day without wine or sunshine. Some of us were born into a Christian community, most of us were born into communities influenced by the Christian community's words. Words are our community's symbols, they contain our community within their structure, sound, and memory. Our words belong to us, because we belong to our community. They not only convey meaning, they hold within themselves a lot of our community's faith, history, and values. Between their lines, hidden within their letters, they contain a surplus of meaning, more than we can say when we use them. As the scientist and philosopher Michael Polanyi said, we know more than we can say, and what we cannot say is more important than what we can say. With imagination we can make discoveries in the surplus of meaning in our community words, some of which are ecological.

A community word, which we keep alive in an age of 'Sunday shopping', is sabbath (Gen 2:2). Sabbath denotes God's day; it connotes community prayer, rest for animals and people, and fields, recuperation of the earth, and families together. Sabbath, as a community word, possesses us. Sabbath reminds us that the earth does not belong to us, we belong to the earth. Sabbath connotes our future: resurrection, everlasting life, new creation, eternal rest. In the fourth century, St Basil of Caesarea said, 'This day is, in fact, also the eighth day and it symbolises the fullness that will follow the present time, the day that never closes . . . the age that will never end' (*On the Holy Spirit*, 27). Sir Edwin Hoskins, renowned biblical scholar, once asked, 'Can we rescue a word and discover a universe?' By indwelling the sabbath word, we may discover a universe.

Another community word is manger (*phatne*). The Jewish scriptures, like the Gospels, associate mangers with domestic animals, especially the companionable ox and ass, who make living on the land possible, even enjoyable (Is 1:3; Lk 2:7). Manger also connotes animal intelligence. Animals know their owner, and their manger. In the Lucan infancy story, Jesus, wrapped in swaddling clothes, is laid in a manger, where musicians, poets, artists, and all of us find him with his parents, and the animals. In his maturity, Jesus too associated the manger word with the ox and ass, 'Does not each of you on the sabbath untie his ox or his ass from the manger, and lead it away to water it?' (Lk 13:15). Since St Francis of Assisi's living créche at Greccio, possibly the most influential sermon ever preached, the animals have their place, with Jesus, in Christmas cribs, in homes, churches, schools, market squares, shops, in the créche industry of Naples, and the simple olive wood cribs carved by Palestinian Christians. As T. S. Eliot said, 'The communication of the dead is tongued with fire beyond the language of the living.' Thanks to our ancestors, the manger word connotes ecology. It is a word to which they, and we, belong.

The church's memory of Jesus, including his familiarity with animals, is like an inexhaustible fountain, from which our predecessors, we ourselves, and our descendants, drink deeply, and find refreshment. In community words, such as sabbath and manger, God's Spirit communicates more than the language of the living. The Spirit hides many meanings, said Bernard of Clairvaux, 'under the exterior guise of the letter.'

Creeds as Hedges
We condense our memory of Jesus, in community words, in our creeds. People sometimes wonder if creeds are outdated in a post-modern age of 'choice'. But creeds, like trees, are protective. Our beautiful, carefully wrought community creeds are helpful guides to our identity. Like whitethorn hedges, they show me where I can walk, and, without trespassing, I can plant fruit and grow vegetables. When we pray our creeds, we sometimes discover resident wrens and goldfinches within their protective branches. The 'orthodoxy' of our community creeds, like a good hedge, is both permanently reliable and at the same time needs pruning and shaping, adapting to strange winds, new questions, including, in our time of planetary deterioration, ecological questions. When we sometimes get lost or confused in a post-modern terrain we can find our way home by following the hedges, which never mislead us, but rather point ahead, beyond themselves. Raymond Brown writes: '"Orthodoxy", then, is not always the possession of those who try to hold on to the past. One may find a truer criterion in the direction toward which Christian thought has been tending, even if that direction suggests that past formulations of truth have to be considered inadequate to answer new questions.'[12]

Our creeds, like finely crafted poetry, brim with meaning,

they abound with pictures, metaphors, symbols, even rhythm. Creeds do more than state beliefs -- they glorify God. Their ecological glory is within, and beneath, the protective branches, especially in the tacit and implicit. When we glorify God in our creeds, we celebrate salvation ecology. We profess God, Creator of all things visible and invisible, and God's Word become flesh, embodied and embedded within our earth community; we profess that, in Jesus crucified and risen, the whole earth community, including, we may add, the hedge communities, is reconciled to God. Catechisms are not creeds. But good catechisms can explain creeds. The Catholic Catechism, in a good ecological passage, draws out much that is implicit in our creeds:

> God wills the interdependence of creatures. The sun and the moon, the cedar and the little flower, the eagle and the sparrow: the spectacle of their countless diversities and inequalities tells us that no creature is self-sufficient. Creatures exist only in dependence on each other, to complete each other, in the service of each other.

(*Catechism of the Catholic Church*, 340)

In other words we pray our creeds on behalf of the cosmos. As Nicholas Berdyaev writes, 'It is in the Church that the grass grows, and the flowers blossom, for the Church is nothing less than the cosmos Christianised.'[13] In March primroses, and sometimes wild daffodils, glow brightly beneath whitethorn hedges. Our creeds, and community prayers, are like golden wild flowers pointing ahead. They help us watch our language about God -- and discover in Jesus, Creator and Lord of the cosmos, the Reconciler of heaven and earth.

The Living Law of Prayer

Our services, especially baptism and the eucharist, testify to all that we, in our cosmos, are, all that we believe. In our worship we profess faith in salvation of all creation by God, through Jesus. Orthodox theologian Myroslav Tataryn writes, 'A positive view of creation is seen not only in the tradition of theological reflection which we find in the Fathers, but also in the liturgical sacramental tradition. In these sources we recognise the belief that Christ saves not only humanity, but also -- through humanity -- the entire created order.' In a Catholic eucharist we pray, 'all creation rightly gives you praise'; we unite the whole created community, in a cosmic liturgy, making present on our altar tables what Jesus did, and does, for us. In our ancient offertory prayers, tongued with fire, we include grass and flowers, sun and rain, micro-organisms, and all soil creatures which, through human hands, contribute to 'bread which earth has given and human hands have made', and wine, 'fruit of the vine and work of human hands.' We recall 'the new and everlasting covenant', linking our offerings with God's cosmic covenant with Noah's descendants, and the sensate creatures who are our covenant partners (Gen 9:16; Heb 13:20).

On high feasts, Orthodox Christians celebrate an *artaklasia*, or agape meal, asking God's blessing on familiar food and crafts. Fruits of the earth, including bread, wine, olive oil, and wheat, are placed on a table in the middle of the church, with icons, cloth, and candles. A beautiful Jesus centred prayer asks blessings upon the whole earth community, and the cosmos:

O Lord Jesus Christ Our God,
Who blessed the five loaves in the wilderness
And from them satisfied the five thousand,
Yourself bless these loaves, this wheat, and this oil,
And multiply them in this city, and throughout the world,
And sanctify the faithful, who shall eat of them in faith.
For you are the blessing and sanctification of all things,
O Christ, our God,
And to you we ascribe all glory,
Together with your Unoriginate Father,
And your All-Holy, Good, and Life-Giving Spirit:
Now and forever, and to the Ages of Ages, Amen.[14]

We are more aware today of the earth's brokenness, and the need for earth healing and restoration, than were the early Christians who composed our liturgical prayers and services.

The Bishop of Arundel and Brighton, Kieran Conry, said recently in a pastoral letter, 'Life is not confined to human life . . . The beauty of the earth on which God allows us to spend the brief span of our lives, this beauty must be respected and preserved. All life is sacred, and the care of the environment is what God first entrusted to Adam.' A similar example of adapting to our new context, with a more aware and earth inclusive ministry, is a blessing of ordinands by John Hind, Anglican Bishop of Chichester:

> As deacons, you will be people sent on a dusty journey with a message. It is a message about how God has already, in Christ, done all that is necessary to bring in His kingdom. It is our privilege as His ministers to announce that kingdom, and to make it visible in the middle of the course of this world's affairs, especially in the care of the environment and ecology.

The Wells of Theological Art
Theology, like our creeds and rituals, is not the preserve of a few, but flows from the whole Jesus movement. Theologians, poets and artists are a rich source, a precious spring, of insights into earth theology and spirituality. The Lyons theologian and Cardinal, Henri de Lubac, noted the connection between medieval exegesis, or interpretations, of the scriptures, and theological art, 'Medieval exegesis found expression also in art, with a marvellous power and fecundity.' A contemporary, the Dominican theologian M. D. Chenu, agreed that art, no less than written theology, 'is a genuine theological source.' Theological art, and crafts, no less than our creeds, prayers, hymns, and good theology, celebrate God's creation from different perspectives, and with different techniques. All express the faith of the church. Pope John Paul II, himself an accomplished poet, dramatist, and crafter of eloquent ecological homilies, said, 'No matter the style, sacred art must express the faith and hope of the church . . . the artist must realise he is doing a service to the church.'

When I have a free day in cities, I try to visit museums, especially exhibitions, and study theological masterpieces with insights into salvation ecology. Artists, including brilliant craftsmen and women, uncover treasures in God's word that academic theologians sometimes skate over obliviously. When living in Ripon, I had literally on my doorstep the work of a famed Renaissance school of carvers, which peaked in the fifteenth century, in the master craftsman William Bromflet, or, as he was sometimes called, Carver. The Ripon School did misericords at Ripon, Beverley, Manchester, and Bridlington Priory. At Ripon they carved Caleb and Joshua, carrying lush grapes from the promised land, symbolising 'Christ the Cluster', with ecological connotations of the fertile land of grapes, springs, olives, milk, and honey, and of the Last Supper, the cosmic cross, and the eucharist. They also carved Samson, absconding with the gates of Gaza, a symbol of Jesus harrowing Hades, in the completeness of victory over death, and of universal salvation. There are also two misericords of Jonah, symbolising Jesus' burial in the depths of the earth, and the resurrection. The Ripon carvers also portrayed the green man, on misericords, and on the choir screen. There are two other Ripon green men, carved in stone, one inside the cathedral west entrance, and, more famously, one grimacing just outside the chapel of nine altars at Fountains Abbey. The Fountains green man, expelled from church, faces east, the direction of sunrise, paradise, resurrection. Both those carved in wood and those in stone appear uncomfortable, as if realising their hour is past. Or do they warn of the folly of polytheism? Or nature worship? The green men, and jacks in the green, scattered around Yorkshire pubs, seem cheerful and bright. The Ripon green men are sombre and dark. As C. S. Lewis remarked, 'holy places are dark places.' The Ripon green men are darkly companionable, but not adorable.

In more intimate ways than in minsters and abbeys, medieval craftsmen celebrated salvation ecology throughout Europe. A well visited 'five star' example – and there are many such – is Fairford Parish Church, Gloucestershire, for Fairford,

almost alone among English country churches, escaped the
Puritan glass smashers, England's indigenous iconoclasts.
'Fairford is like a vast illuminated missal', writes Simon Jenkins
in his delightful tour of English churches.[15] At Fairford, John
Keble, later an early light in the Oxford Movement, and
Professor of Poetry at Oxford, grew up in his father's rectory,
and worshipped in the illuminated church. When we pause quietly at the Fairford windows, we notice that the Fairford glaziers
related family life to the incarnation. Saints Ann and Joachim are
there, as parents of Mary and grandparents of the Word made
flesh. Mary and Joseph are portrayed in scenes before and after
Jesus' birth, and in scenes from his boyhood. The family donkey,
with the ox, is present at the manger, and again on the flight to
Egypt, as are the flora and fauna of the wilderness. In a humbler,
more local way than the craftsmen of the mighty minsters, the
medieval glaziers at Fairford, in Flanders, and throughout
Europe, complement the carvers and masons, together sharing
in a cosmic liturgy.

Some favourite themes of theological art are creation, the
Fall, Noah, the Annunciation, the Nativity and flight, the baptism, the miracles, the Last Supper, the crucifixion and resurrection, the death and assumption of Mary, and, frequently in the
western portals of church, the Last Judgement and Christ reigning as Pantocrator, Creator of all that is. When we make connections, with imagination, these scenes and themes contribute to
earth spirituality, and cosmic liturgy. So does theological poetry,
of which I select two favourites here. One is a description by the
Orkney poet, Edwin Muir, of Jesus' birth, life and death:

Was born a Child in body bound
Among the cattle in a byre.
The clamorous world was all around,
Beast, insect, plant, earth, water, fire.

On bread and wine his flesh grew tall,
The round sun helped him on his way,
Wood, iron, herb and animal
His friends were till the testing day.

Then braced by iron and by wood,
Engrafted on a tree he died,
And little dogs lapped up the blood
That spurted from his broken side.
(Thought and Image)

The Irish poet and farmer, Patrick Kavanagh, discovered traces of the Trinity, especially in April, in the stony grey soil of his north facing fields, in Monaghan. Kavanagh discovered God's presence, the Father, and Creator, in small things of the earth, in 'yellow flame blossom of the whin', and in 'seed like stars against the black eternity of April clay'. Kavanagh, who had little formal schooling, in his 'unlibraried fields' pondered his confirmation lessons all his life, and found the Holy Spirit in trees and hills. Of himself Kavanagh wrote:

The Holy Ghost was taking the Bedlam of the little fields and making it into a song, a simple song which he could understand. And he saw the Holy Spirit on the hills.

With the cynical side of himself, he realised that there was nothing unusual about the landscape. And yet what he imagined was hardly self-deception. The totality of the scene about him was a miracle. There might be something of self-deception in his imagination of the general landscape but there was none in his observation of the little flowers and weeds. These had God's message in them.[16]

The author of the Wisdom of Solomon, composed near the time when Jesus walked the earth, found evidence of God in the beauty of the earth, as did Patrick Kavanagh, and scores of poets, artists, and environmentalists through the centuries, 'the greatness and beauty of created things gives us a corresponding idea of their Creator' (Wis 13:5). In words often quoted, and pondered by Christian writers and thinkers, St Paul clearly agreed, 'What can be known about God is plain to them, because God has shown it to them. Ever since the creation of the world his invisible nature, namely, his eternal power and deity, has been clearly perceived in the things that have been made' (Rom 1:19-20). The 'things that have been made' also remind us of

Christ, God's Word, in whom 'all things' were made, and especially his death and resurrection, reconciling the cosmos. All
things, 'united not absorbed', are included in salvation. An
Orthodox monk writes:

> You are looking at the sun? Then think of Him who is the
> Light of the World, albeit shrouded in darkness. You are
> looking at the trees and their branches growing green again
> each spring? Then think of Him who, hanging on the wood
> of the cross, draws everything to himself. You are looking at
> rocks and stones? Then think of the stone in the garden that
> was blocking the entrance to a tomb. That stone was rolled
> away and since then the door of the sepulchre has never been
> shut.[17]

God is vividly present in the planets, in 'seed like stars', and in
the myriad biodiverse 'things that have been made'. As an amateur food grower, I am annually astonished, like Kavanagh, by
the incredible, except that it is real, miracle of fruit appearing
and swelling and colouring on trees. April buds and blossoms,
then developing into fruitlets, swelling and growing and eventually ripening into sweetness. All this on trees, the perennial
Christian symbol of the cross. Another miracle happens when a
tiny tomato seed, held gingerly in my hand, and sown into organic compost indoors in April, becomes a scrambling, blossoming, fruiting Yellow Ripple Currant tomato vine. Those tiny
seeds, saved in November, and sown in my study in April, ger-
minate quickly in the warmth, grow swiftly, demand pricking
out, and repotting, and transplanting into their natural habitat
outdoors, where, until November, they burst with health and
vigour and currant sized tomatoes, finally resowing themselves
in the cooling soil. All this floral and food diversity from the
barely visible seed, in my hand, in April! 'Seed like stars, against
the black eternity of April clay', wrote Kavanagh. Sowing seeds
organically, a person feels religious about nature.

Conclusion
Which brings me to the conclusion of 'our way of proceeding', a

way that culminates in practice. As we contemplate the whole, many-splendoured and living Christian reality, from before the Christian scriptures were composed to our recent theological artists and poets, we make startling, even thrilling, discoveries. Within that living Christian tradition, that memory of Christ in the Church community, are our sisters and brothers who are environmentalists, who love God's earth, live sustainably locally, and inspire us with their practice. We can learn from these people who successfully correlate their commitment to Jesus with commitment to our earth. Many of them have inspired me, personally and profoundly, some are quoted in this book. Within our environmentally deteriorating post-modern time, in continuity with the ascetic wilderness tradition, the early Franciscans, and scores of missionaries and rural Christians, we can draw inspiration from recent, and contemporary, Christian environmentalists. For many, these would include John Muir, Fritz Schumacher, Barbara Ward, Norman Moore, Jane Goodall, and countless more. I conclude this chapter with nearly 'last word' words of John Seymour, who has inspired and encouraged me, as have few others, and whose writings, in the words of Countryfile's John Craven, 'have influenced millions'. John Seymour's own profound earth spirituality always included practice, on many fronts, including broadcasting, writing widely read books and articles, lecturing, campaigning, even, in his eighties, destroying, 'in self-defence', genetically mutilated sugar beets. 'An insult to the Creation', said John, 'is an insult to the Creator'. In widely quoted words, John writes:

> The tiny amount you and I can do is hardly likely to bring the huge worldwide Moloch of plundering industry down? Well if you and I don't do it, it will not be done. We have to do it – just the two of us – just you and me. There is no 'them' – there is nobody else. Just you and me. On our infirm shoulders we must take up this heavy burden now: the task of restoring the health, the wholeness, the beauty and the integrity of our planet. We must start the Age of Healing now! Tomorrow will be too late.[18]

Notes:
1. Mark Allen Powell, *The Jesus Debate, Modern Historians Investigate the Life of Christ* (Oxford: Lion, 1998), p. 195.
2. Edwin Le Grice, *Sharp Reflections, Poems of Faith* (Rottesden: Kevin Mayhew Ltd, 1993), preface.
3. In Paul Brown, 'Sermon on the cruise ship', ('Society', *The Guardian* (19 June 2002), p. 8.
4. Ignatius Loyola, *The Text of the Spiritual Exercises of Saint Ignatius*, John Morris SJ (ed) (Maryland: Newman Press, 1949), pp. 24-25.
5. Powell, *The Jesus Debate*, p. 196.
6. John Anthony McGuckin, *Standing in God's Holy Fire, the Byzantine Tradition* (London: Darton, Longman & Todd, 2001), p. 77.
7. Jean Danielou, *The Bible and the Liturgy* (London: Darton Longman & Todd, 1956), p. 17.
8. M. Francis Mannion, 'Bringing the Cosmos to the Liturgy', *Second Spring*, 2 (2002), p. 55.
9. Leonardo Boff, *Saint François d'Assisi* (Cerf, 1986), p. 67.
10. Ignatius Loyola, *Spiritual Exercises*, p. 36.
11. John Henry Newman, *Essay in Aid of a Grammar of Assent* (Indiana: University of Notre Dame Press, 1979), p. 89.
12. Raymond E. Brown, *The Community of the Beloved Disciple* (New York: Paulist Press, 1979), pp. 80-81.
13. Nicholas Berdyaev, *Freedom and the Spirit* (London: Geoffrey Bles, 1935), p. 351.
14. McGuckin, *Standing in God's Holy Fire*, p. 144.
15. Simon Jenkins, *England's Thousand Best Churches* (London: Penguin Press, 1999), p. 215.
16. Patrick Kavanagh, *Tarry Flynn* (London: Penguin Books, 1978), pp. 29-30; cf. Una Agnew, *The Mystical Imagination of Patrick Kavanagh: A Buttonhole in Heaven?* (Dublin: The Columba Press, 1998), p. 197.
17. A Monk of the Eastern Church, *Love without Limits* (Chevetogne, 1971), pp. 27-28.
18. John Seymour, 'The Age of Healing', *Green Christians*, 48 (Spring 2002), p. 20; cf also 'The Age of Healing' (poem) *Green Christian*, 54 (Spring 2004), p. 9.

CHAPTER THREE

What Good Can Come Out of Nazareth?

Has not the scripture said that the Christ
is descended from David, and comes from Bethlehem?

(Jn 7:42)

In their infancy narratives, the gospels of both Matthew and
Luke record that Jesus was born in Bethlehem of Judea, David's
city. Both also agree that he grew up a good way north of
Bethlehem, in the small, fertile village of Nazareth of Galilee.
There Jesus lived most of his relatively short life, making that
obscure village famous. Our four gospels tell us remarkably little
about Nazareth, or Jesus' Nazareth years. Other, 'apocryphal' –
or not accepted as fully reliable – gospels are less reticent. They
describe in some detail Jesus' boyhood years, his friendship
with his cousin John, his family life, and some improbable miracles he is alleged to have performed as a child. Nevertheless,
from some reliable clues in our four canonical – or accepted –
gospels, from the Jewish scriptures, from contemporary Jewish
and Hellenic writings, and from archaeology and ecology, we
get some idea of Jesus' formative years in 'his own country'.

Nazareth is not only important for Jesus' own formation, it is
important – more than most modern spirituality realises – for
our own relationships with him. As a boy, in my own formative
years, and in a milieu different from Galilee, I learned from my
parents, and from the Sisters and lay teachers at Gesu school,
that Jesus grew up and played at Nazareth, like other boys, and
at times probably visited his near relatives. We did not learn
then that Jesus almost certainly had brothers and sisters. It was
widely assumed, including in some scholarly circles, that Jesus
was an only child with cousins. I still remember with appreciation the haunting words of a gentle children's hymn, taught to

us by the IHM Sisters, and sung in May, which was Mary's month. A lifetime later the words, and the melody, linger on:

Lovely Lady dressed in blue,
Teach me how to pray!
God was just your little boy,
Tell me what to say!

We learned that, although he was God, Jesus learned from his parents who were his teachers and from his elders. Nor did he remain a small boy. In one of several mentions of Nazareth, Luke says he increased 'in age, wisdom and grace' before God and people. With clues like these, and with the perceptive power of imagination, we can draw much 'fruit', that is we can grasp in our hearts what Jesus was and did and even what he thought about his Father's will for him at, and after, Nazareth. I have known, and still meet today, young women and men who leave home, family, and friends to follow Jesus intensely. I suspect that some of their generosity – and the good they do – derives from imaginative contemplation of Jesus in his Nazareth years. As Newman said, 'the heart is commonly reached, not through the reason, but the imagination.' When we contemplate Jesus as a youth, in the green hills of Nazareth, we sometimes gain insights into his ecology, his connectedness with other beings, his familiarity with the ways of family fields. We see in the Nazareth years not only salvation history, but salvation ecology as well. Jesus of Nazareth is the 'first born of all creation' living within our earth community, destined to share our common future (Col 1:10). Olivier Clement stretches us when he writes, 'the Word, by becoming incarnate, has reopened for us the paradisal dimension of the world. Opaque but transparent, the earth is the paradise which we can re-enter by dying and rising with Christ.'[1] Jesus, like ourselves, was interrelated to the earth creatures around him, and they to him. In those formative years, he learned about the soil creatures which illustrate his parables, and which share in our redemption.

Considering that the village was the boyhood, and early manhood, home of the most important person in human history, it is surprising how little is recoverable of pre-historic Nazareth, and the people who lived there, some of whom cultivated the fields which later belonged to Jesus' family. Even in our four gospels, Nazareth is mentioned only twelve times. In the Jewish scriptures, and in Hebrew literature, it is not noticed at all. The earliest post-biblical reference is by Julian Africanus, in AD 221.[2] It appears even later in Hebrew writings, as 'Nasrat', in the eighth century.[3] Nevertheless, when we consider the dates of Herod the Great, Tiberius, and Pontius Pilate, we can estimate that Jesus lived at Nazareth from about 6 BC to AD 30. Of that thirty-six or so years of his earthly life, Jesus lived all but about two in Nazareth. He was, and remained, so much a part of Nazareth, that 'of Nazareth', Nazarene, or Nazorean, became virtually his second name. 'Of Nazareth' appears on a cross from the most important tree in the history of planet earth (Jn 19:19). In the fourth gospel there is an ironic allusion to Nazareth. When he was teaching in Jerusalem, the Jews queried his origins: 'Some of the people said, "This is really the prophet." Others said, "This is the Christ." But some said, "Is the Christ to come from Galilee? Has not the scripture said that the Christ is descended from David, and comes from Bethlehem, the village where David was?"' (Jn 7:40-43).

The authors and readers of John's gospel, which include ourselves, know that Jesus was indeed of David, and therefore of Bethlehem, and also much more, the Christ from Galilee, God's Word in whom all things are created, God himself (Jn 1:2).

Birth in Bethlehem

What then of Bethlehem, the 'little town' we celebrate so movingly in our Christmas carol? The Christmas story, and that particular carol, are so familiar and Luke so clear about the journey Mary and Joseph took to Bethlehem and what happened at the manger, that it is surprising how little interest the gospels show in David's city. None describe Jesus as 'of Bethlehem', or 'a Bethlehemite'; he is 'of Nazareth', or 'a Nazarene'. Yet Matthew agrees with Luke that Jesus was born of the Virgin Mary, in the

Davidic town of Bethlehem. Indeed, according to Matthew, Bethlehem was Mary and Joseph's home town. It was to Bethlehem, Matthew says, that the star and the Magi came. Nazareth became the family home, because after the sojourn in Egypt, Mary and Joseph feared to return to Bethlehem, while Herod Archelaus ruled Judea. Matthew adds that the move to Nazareth fulfils the Jewish scriptures that the Messiah would be 'a Nazarene'. There are ecological echoes in Matthew's references, for the Isaiah text he cites refers to the awaited peaceable kingdom (Is 11:1-9; Mt 2:23). With imagination we can certainly make the connection, as do many Christmas services, and readings: Jesus is the Prince of Peace for all creation. Luke agrees that, despite the Bethlehem birth, the holy family were Nazarenes. In Luke's account Jesus was born in Bethlehem because a census summoned Joseph, a Davidean, to David's city where Jesus was born and laid in a manger, with its connotations of peace with the animals (Lk 2:7; Is 1:3). Luke says that after visiting the Jerusalem Temple the family returned to Nazareth. Both Matthew and Luke, therefore, in their different ways, agree that Jesus was both of Bethlehem and of Nazareth. Mark's gospel, which has no infancy account, describes Nazareth as Jesus' 'own country' (his home town!). John's irony, as we have seen, connects Jesus with both towns (Mk 6:1; Jn 7:40-42).

Nazareth Life

Jesus' young mother, Mary, was probably in her teens, perhaps as young as fifteen, when Jesus was born. Despite my boyhood impression, it seems that Jesus did not grow up as an only child. According to both Mark and Matthew, he had four brothers and some sisters (Mk 6:3; Mt 13:55-56). Mark says that, like Joseph, he was a craftsman, a *tekton*, what today we might call a carpenter, although with different skills for a bioregion in which wood was scarce. Trees feature throughout Jesus' life. We could paraphrase what the African lawyer and apologist, Tertullian, says about Jesus and water, by saying Jesus is never without trees! Their relative scarcity at Nazareth, where wood was used mainly for infrastructure, doors, and windows of buildings, inclined people to appreciate wood, including prunings from fruit trees and vines. Craftsmen in Galilee approximate what today we call middle class. The rich, or upper, class, were Herod Antipas and his officials, rich merchants, large, often absentee, landowners, and senior tax collectors. The middle class, to which Jesus' family belonged, consisted of freeholders, with a reasonable share, or *nahalah*, of God's land, craftsmen such as Joseph and Jesus, and successful businessmen. The middle class was vulnerable to the vagaries of weather, harvests, supply and demand, inflation, and taxes, both civil and religious. As a middle-class son of a large family, Jesus almost certainly supplemented his family's income by growing food on family land. A few, inalienable, fields, with livestock and fruit trees, enabled middle-class farmers to be partly self-sufficient – and gave them an attachment to, and appreciation of the soil. There is archaeological evidence of terraces, and olive presses, in iron age Nazareth. Some of Jesus' family fields were probably soil and moisture retentive terraces.[4] Beneath the middle class were the labourers, the landless poor, including servants, casual labourers, travellers, dispossessed farmers, bandits, and slaves.[5] If there were just two classes in Galilee, then craftsmen were near the middle of the lower class. *All* classes, upper, middle, and poor, despite inherent and culturally determined stratifications, were in solidarity, united in their shared dependence on the sun, rainfall, precious trees and shade, soil fertility, and biodiversity of Galilee.[6] As Jesus observed then and later, God's rain falls on just and unjust.

Education

We know little about the Nazareth synagogue which Jesus attended as a youth. It may not have been purpose built, but a room above a community leader's house. There is a synagogue in Nazareth old town today, but we cannot be certain it is on the same site or foundations where Jesus studied, worshipped, and, as a young man, read and preached. The same building may have served as residence, school, and synagogue. In any case the Nazareth synagogue had an uncommon worshipper! John

Meier, who specialises in historical Jesus studies, suggests that 'One and the same person might have served as servant of the synagogue, scribe and elementary school teacher.'[7] Such a village scribe, or schoolmaster, would have instructed Jesus and other boys in the Books of Moses, some prophetic writings, and possibly some Hebrew. Jesus also heard – and learned from – homilies after readings in the synagogue. We notice in the gospels his familiarity with some important ecological texts in the Jewish writings, or 'scriptures', including the creation accounts, Isaiah, the Psalms, legislation protecting wild and domestic animals, and the Book of Daniel. Yale University's Harry Gamble, an authority on first-century literacy, argues that villages such as Nazareth did have elementary schools connected with the synagogue, where pupils learned basic reading skills and studied the Hebrew Torah.[8] Jesus was observant of the natural world, and, as a young reader, he chose holistic texts from the Isaiah writings for a reading in the synagogue (Lk 4:18-19).

We sometimes wonder – and I certainly am asked! – about the real Jesus and modern environmental problems, like deforestation and climate change; did he realise the connection between human actions and climate change, erosion, drought, floods, and extinctions? In a sense yes, but also no, because these problems had barely surfaced in Jesus' time, although unsustainable deforestation around the Mediterranean had begun. We just noticed his close observation of the natural world in Nazareth, especially in his own family fields. He also knew, from school, the perennial ecological wisdom of the Torah and the Jewish writings, and the wisdom of sabbath rest for land and animals as well as people. There was then – and still is – a perennial relevance, now more than ever, of Deuteronomy 11:

> If you will obey my commandments which I command you this day, to love the Lord your God, and to serve him with all your heart and with all your soul, he will give the rain for your land in its season, the early rain and the later rain, that you may gather in your grain and your wine and your oil. And he will give grass in your fields for your cattle, and you

shall eat and be full. Take heed lest your heart be deceived, and you turn aside and serve other gods and worship them, and the anger of the Lord be kindled against you, and he shut up the heavens, so that there be no rain, and the land yield no fruit, and you perish quickly off the good land which the Lord gives you (Deut 11:13-17).

Luke, who was especially interested in the Nazareth years, says Jesus was 'subject' to his parents, using a Greek word that from the context means voluntary subjection, including instruction, and learning of hereditary wisdom. His primary teachers of religion, morality, and the environment were his parents; his primary school, the home. His family's observations, and experiences, of nature, complemented the sometimes detailed observations in the scriptures. From his mother Jesus probably learned about living beings in Nazareth, such as insects, spiders, and larger creatures, and plants, inhabiting the few 'open spaces' within the settlement, and the wildlife moving on the edges, and occasionally venturing inwards as they do to this day. Even now, in that tense and overcrowded town, I have noticed a variety of cultivated and wild life. To mention a few, there are cultivated fruit trees, vegetables, and vines, flowers, elder, brambles, migrant birds, raptors, and sparrows, grasses, wild flowers, mallow, stinging nettles, Tabor oak, cypresses, figs, olives, and domestic animals. Galilee air space enjoys the migrations of birds flying north in spring and south in autumn. These and other living wonders Jesus discovered and studied with his young mother and siblings, within the white walls of Nazareth. The children's hymn I learned as a schoolboy contains some high christology, and implicitly teaches respect for God's earth: 'Lovely Lady, dressed in blue, teach me how to pray. God was just your little boy. Tell me what to say.'

The Nazareth Soil Community

As John Seymour says, a biosystem is a soil community in which we, the dominant species, are soil organisms. When we observe the variety of soil community members, both wild and cultivated,

in Jesus' parables, and when we consider the still remaining fertility in crowded Nazareth today, we can, with the perceptive
and connective power of imagination, contemplate the maturing
Jesus in a very biodiverse habitat. With good reason, the site was
occupied by stone-age and later people for about 1500 years before Jesus lived, learned, and grew food in its environs. The village was roughly fifteen miles from Lake Galilee, and about
twenty from the sea. It huddles snuggly in a protected basin, facing south-east, about 1400 feet above sea level, within the fertile
upper reaches of the green hills of lower Galilee. The village, in
Jesus' time, accommodated about 2000 people, with their domestic animals, covering about 40,000 square metres. Below
stretches the fertile Esdraleon plain and, in the distance, Megiddo.
Below Nazareth, to the south-east is Nain. From the shade of an
olive grove at Nain, near the ruins of the Roman gate where,
says Luke, Jesus met a Nain widow and raised her son, I have
for several hours watched the sun move across Nazareth (Lk
7:12). The spring sun saturates the Nazareth basin, its houses,
gardens, olives, figs, and vines. Jesus would have appreciated
shade, sometimes found only near a large rock, a fig, an olive,
the way an English or Irish person appreciates sun in daffodil
and blackthorn time, after a long winter.

The soil fertility and biodiversity of Nazareth was as familiar
to Jesus as are sidewalks to mayors of New York. And it is a lush
community he knew. The Jewish historian Josephus (b. AD 37),
who just missed being a younger contemporary of Jesus, knew
Galilee well, for during the Jewish revolt of AD 66-70 he was a
commander there. He later wrote of the Galilee where Jesus
spent almost his entire life:

> The whole area is excellent for crops or cattle and rich in
> forests of every kind, so that by its adaptability it invites even
> those least inclined to work on the land. Consequently every
> inch has been cultivated by the inhabitants and not a corner
> goes to waste.[9]

The defences a desperate people use when besieged testify to
their poverty and also to the fertility of the land they defend. At

the Galilee town of Jotapata, about six miles north-west of Nazareth, the Jewish defenders poured scalding oil on their assailants, a defence mechanism that demonstrates ingenuity – and the abundance of olives in lower Galilee: 'Josephus, taught by necessity – always quick to improvise when despair applies the spur – ordered boiling oil to be poured on the soldiers under the shields. As his men had it ready, numbers of them from every side poured quantities of it on the Romans, followed by the vessels still hissing from the flames.'[10] Not surprisingly, archaeological excavations in Nazareth in the 1950s discovered olive presses and vats, as well as millstones, silos, and water cisterns.

Jewish family fields were virtually inalienable, similar to *campos* around the Mediterranean today. Jewish wisdom and their scriptures endorsed this wise custom as God-given. People do tenderly care for a piece of land when it 'belongs' to them, and is not leased. Near Jesus' time, the poet Horace wrote, 'This was among my desires, a piece of field not too large, suitable for a garden; and next to the house a spring of living water; and in addition, a small woodland.' And the Mosaic law says wisely, 'In the inheritance which you will hold in the land that the Lord your God gives you to possess, you shall not remove your neighbour's landmark, which the men of old have set' (Deut 19:14). Later the compiler of Proverbs repeated this Jewish tradition, 'Do not remove an ancient landmark or enter the fields of the fatherless' (Prov 23:10; 1 Kgs 21:3). Centuries later, in Ireland, Daniel O'Connell, 'the Liberator' by peaceful means, quoted this scriptural wisdom.

In Nazareth fields, olive plantations, sometimes on terraces, as well as solitary trees in fields, provided broken shade. With their rugged, probing roots, olives, like comfrey, draw minerals from sub-soil, depositing them on the surface through leaf fall. Olives shade and shelter stock, who return the favour by depositing manure near the trees. The leaves provide cooling relief, and shelter, in the long, intense growing season, when families work the fields. Their roots assist permeability in winter.

Families harvest olives by spreading blankets beneath the trees, and by picking or 'beating' the green and black fruit from the branches. Picking times, and recipes for preserving olives, vary. Those without trees of their own can purchase or barter olives at market. In Jesus' time, men pollarded mature trees, feeding leaves to animals, and recycling branches in winter fires. Larger branches served as wood, for window and door frames, and for furniture. Men returned ashes and 'dust' to the soil, as part of the organic circle of recycled fertility. Nazareth was a circular, and not a linear, organism. John's gospel shows Jesus' intimate familiarity with fruit, and the inclusion of fruit in the local organic circle (Jn 15:2, 6). This circle was the local, organic, sustainable, biodiverse, 'dry' horticulture in which Jesus participated. The rural imagery which makes his parables so memorable was drawn from the village life he and his hearers understood. Jesus was able to use familiar rural metaphors and symbols – look especially at Mark 4 and Matthew 13, sometimes called 'the green chapters' – because of the diverse creatures and the horticulture he describes. Jesus and his neighbours shared precious springs, irrigation channels, olive presses, vats, silos, threshing floors, ovens, and the market place. Jesus was more than a one-craft craftsman, he was also akin to what we would call a small-holder, or allotment gardener. John Meier writes:

> In the gospels Jesus is nowhere portrayed as a farmer. To be sure, Jesus and the rest of his family may have been engaged in part-time farming of some plot of land. The size of the family (Joseph, Mary, Jesus, four brothers of Jesus, and an undetermined number of sisters) would argue for both the need and the ability of his family unit to provide at least some of its food from farming – as one would expect anyway in the case of villagers close to the fertile slopes and fields of Lower Galilee. This may help explain – though only in part – why a good deal of the imagery in Jesus' parables and metaphorical language is taken from agriculture rather than from the workshop.[11]

Jesus' community, however, also rested. Sabbath, for people and land, and animals, is, and was, a recurrent teacher, not an inflexible judge. Even on the sabbath, Galilee Jews watered and fed their animals. The sabbath was for people and their soil community, not people for the sabbath. 'Does not each of you on the sabbath untie his ox or his ass from the manger, and lead it away to water it? ... Which of you, having a son or an ox that has fallen into a well, will not immediately pull him out on a sabbath day?' (Lk 13:15; 14:5).

When winter rains softened, and ceased, and golden spring crept over the hills, Jesus probably joined other villagers, harvesting barley, spring herbs, and other 'free food' such as dandelions, and young nettles, and the much valued delicious 'early figs' (Micah 7:1).[12] Early spring was also sowing time, for cereals and vegetables. Jesus and his family saved and stored seed, and sowed their fields, centuries before Jethro Tull's mechanised seed drill, scattering their carefully saved seed by hand, as in the parable of the sower (Mk 4:3-9). Seed falling on friable soil, watered by the soft rain, and prepared by manual cultivation, soon germinated, and became palpably living plants. At summer harvest, families selected seeds from favoured plants, and saved them for next spring's sowing. Jesus and his extended family anticipated modern heritage seed savers around the world. Families select, sow, and pass on precious, well adapted seeds, which, like favourite animals, become part of a family. We may wonder if cereal genes, from seeds selected and saved by Jesus, have come down to us in our daily bread. Our seeds, and crops and bread, are from God, on earth as in heaven!

Jesus understood the value of compost, mostly animal and fowl manure, which was moisture retentive and conditioned soil for the early autumn and spring rains. Compost becomes humus and nurtures plants. Compost mulch preserves moisture and suppresses weeds around figs, vines, and other fruit, and with the co-operation of micro-organisms nourishes feeder roots beneath (Lk 13:8-9). Figs, grapes, and pomegranates were staple fruits, but there were others including brambles, and even apples. According to Josephus, Herod the Great liked peeled apples,

and requested some on his death bed.[13] Another historian,
Eusebius of Caesarea, in the fourth century, reports an anecdote
of Hegesippus, a second-century Palestinian Christian, and contemporary of the collateral descendants of Jesus. According to
Hegesippus, Emperor Domitian, suspicious of anyone of
Davidic lineage, summoned two grandsons of Jesus' brother
Jude. They testified that they worked a small plot of land, similar to what we would call a small-holding. What is of interest,
whether or not the story is legendary, is that Palestinians, such
as Hegesippus, and later Eusebius of Caesarea, thought it natural
for Jesus' collateral descendants to work the land; and that they
were not described as craftsmen. The account also shows that
there were traditions of food growing in Jesus' family.[14]

Nazareth Earth Spirituality
Except for roughly two years, Jesus' entire life was lived in the
Galilean hill country. Here he learned from his parents and elders, and from his own observations, about the organic soil
community, its fragility, needs, biodiversity, and awesome generosity. To express this learning experience in another way, it
was in the fertile fields of Nazareth that Jesus learned to love the
soil community, created and redeemed in him. In his remembered parables, we hear, and visually imagine, his Nazarene
familiarity with winter rains, wind, wheat and tares, figs and
vines, wild and domestic animals, manure, and especially remembered, and repeated in pictorial arts, the world of seeds,
their origins, their sowing, and their ways. His metaphors are
not elaborated, for his immediate hearers and ourselves, from
preachers' manuals. He was a highly gifted genius, a 'gem of
purest ray serene', who from his own experience knew about
seeds germinating, about small seeds becoming large brassicas,
about plants growing slowly, about what tares did to wheat, and
manure to ailing figs. The late New Testament scholar, C. H.
Dodd, observes, 'Clearly we are in touch with a mind of a poetic
and imaginative cast. This should never be forgotten in any at-
tempt to understand the teaching of Jesus.'[15] When we contem-

plate Jesus in his 'hidden life', we accompany him, imaginatively, in familiar habitats, where he grew up, learned about the earth, and touched and was touched by insects, plants, birds, and villagers. Since then, says St Ninian, pointing to the cosmic Christ, Jesus is 'reflected in every plant and insect, every bird and animal and man and woman'. In the biodiverse fields of Nazareth, Jesus sanctified by his presence all the farms and gardens, fruit and vegetables, animals and rain in the cosmos. All fields are forever the cosmic Nazareth (Eph 1:6-10).

Which brings us to the question of whether Jesus was an organic food grower. In the sense that all food growing in iron age Palestine was free of synthetic chemical input, we may say that Jesus was an organic grower. He and his contemporaries, assisted by donkeys, and their manure, worked with the soil, not against it. They nurtured plants by nourishing the soil. In their fields, and especially on terraces, they grew intensively. A good parallel is our 3 ft by 20 ft organic fruit and vegetable bed today. We avoid heavy machinery and chemical input, we encourage natural predators, such as ladybirds, lacewings, and hedgehogs, we feed the plants by feeding the soil, we harvest rain, we return to the soil, as compost, what plants remove, but we grow food as intensively as some agrochemical barley barons and chemical viticulturists. Organic beds are intensive plots which, unlike chemical plots or fields, are sustainable. When we contemplate – and communicate with – Jesus in the fields of Nazareth, when we employ imagination, Wordsworth's 'auxiliar light', we 'see, hear, and touch' Jesus, not only at the craftsman's bench, but growing organically in green and golden family fields.

Nazareth Homecoming

The gospels narrate several homecomings of Jesus. We can recall Luke's (probably legendary) story of his getting lost in Jerusalem, his being found in the Temple, and his return, with Mary and Joseph and other relatives, from Jerusalem to Nazareth, where he remained until his departure for the wilderness. The synoptic gospels describe another return to Nazareth, as a mature young man engaged in his brief public ministry. They agree that he was coolly received. Mark says his former neighbours asked, rather dismissively, if he were not 'the wood-worker' (*tekton*), and son of Mary, with brothers and sisters in the village. Jesus' riposte is famous: 'a prophet is not without ho-nour, except in his own country, and among his own kin, and in his own house' (Mk 6:4). Matthew says the villagers asked if he were not 'the *son* of the *tekton*', thereby distancing Jesus some-what from the woodworker's trade. The most detailed account of this homecoming, however, is that of Luke which, because of its contemporary ecological and inter-religious relevance, I quote in full:

He came to Nazareth, where he had been brought up; and he went to the synagogue, as his custom was, on the sabbath day. And he stood up to read; and there was given to him the book of the prophet Isaiah. He opened the book and found the place where it was written, 'The Spirit of the Lord is upon me, because he has anointed me to preach good news to the poor. He has sent me to proclaim release to the captives and recovering of sight to the blind, to set at liberty those who are oppressed, to proclaim the acceptable year of the Lord.' And he closed the book, and gave it back to the attendant, and sat down; and the eyes of all in the synagogue were fixed on him. And he began to say to them, 'Today this scripture has been fulfilled in your hearing.' And all spoke well of him, and wondered at the gracious words which proceeded out of his mouth; and they said, 'Is not this Joseph's son?' And he said to them, 'Doubtless you will quote to me this proverb, "Physician, heal yourself; what we have heard you did at Capernaum, do here also in your own country".' And he said, 'Truly, I say to you, no prophet is acceptable in his own country. But in truth, I tell you, there were many widows in Israel in the days of Elijah, when the heaven was shut up three years and six months, when there came a great famine over all the land; and Elijah was sent to none of them but only to Zarephath, in the land of Sidon, to a woman who was a widow. And there were many lepers in Israel in the time of the prophet Elisha; and none of them was cleansed, but only Naaman the Syrian.' When they heard this, all in the synagogue were filled with wrath. And they rose up and put him out of the city, and led him to the brow of the hill on which their city was built, that they might throw him down headlong. But passing through the midst of them he went away (Lk 4:16-30).

The probable order of the synagogue service to which Luke refers was, roughly, a psalm, the Schema (Deut 6:4), eighteen benedictions, readings from the Torah and the prophets, a homily on the readings, a blessing by the president, and a reading of the blessing in Numbers 6:24-27. Luke says Jesus attended these sabbath services and read a lesson. The reading Jesus chose at his homecoming was a combination of Isaiah 61:1-2 and 58:6. The words about the Spirit resting on the Messiah echo Jesus' own baptism, and also Isaiah 11:1. Bishop N. T. Wright comments, 'The passage demands to be read as an echo of e.g. Is 11:1-10.'[16] If Wright is correct, that echo connects Jesus with the peaceable kingdom, wherein the awaited king brings fertility, peace, shalom, with and to all creation, a renewal of paradise. Just as salvation history culminates in Jesus, so does salvation ecology, in which the Nazareth years, not least this Nazareth homecoming as related by Luke, are significant. The Isaiah text, read aloud by Jesus, proclaimed 'release' of debts, which to the Jews evokes jubilee, and the sabbatical year, with release from toil, debts, even prison and, for cultivated soil, rest from cultivated productivity, allowing nature's 'green manure' to restore fertility. Bill McKibben comments, 'The idea of the sabbatical year and the jubilee year have the effect of resting the land and also of preventing the consolidation of the land into what we would now call "agribusiness" farms – the massive industrial spreads that accelerate all the soil erosion and pesticide poisoning and monoculture reliance that are ruining the earth.'[17] We cannot be certain, but Jesus may have intended his first followers to release each *others*' debts, and to live together harmoniously, in what we would call sustainable sufficiency, which is, according to Luke's famous description, what the first Jerusalem community did: 'There was not a needy person among them for as many as were possessors of lands or houses sold them, and brought the proceeds of what was sold and laid it at the apostles' feet' (Acts 4:34-35). Generous sharing, then and now, is countercultural to the human urge to compete, acquire, and consume. Sharing in sustainable sufficiency includes social and ecological justice – for one cannot exist without the other. Jesus would have known Jews who did share possessions, such as urban Essenes, the disciples of the Baptist, and some Pharisee groups. N. T. Wright suggests that jubilee, and Essene-like sharing, was indeed Jesus' intention for his followers:

> If this suggestion is anywhere near the mark, it opens the possibility that, although Jesus did not envisage that he would persuade Israel as a whole to keep the Jubilee year, he expected his followers to live by the Jubilee principle among themselves. He expected, and taught, that they should forgive one another not only 'sins' but also debts. This may help to explain the remarkable practice within the early church whereby resources were pooled, in a fashion not unlike the Essene community of goods. Luke's description of this in Acts 4:34 echoes the description of the sabbatical year in Deuteronomy 15:4.[18]

The Lucan portrayal of Jesus' homecoming includes a final, important, and increasingly relevant part of Jesus' ministry: the inclusion of other races, religions, and world views. Jesus, who went first to 'the lost sheep of the house of Israel', did not exclude, and at times healed and praised, people of other faiths. He was finally rejected at Nazareth, notes Luke, for describing Elijah and Elisha as sent not to heal Jews, but to Sarepath, a gentile widow, and Naaman, a Syrian leper. I believe the importance of inter-religious ecology, for shared sustainability, and for the very continuance of life on earth, has yet to receive the concentrated attention it deserves. I have often experienced what the American philosopher Paul B. Thompson describes: 'Those committed to Judeo-Christian theological ethics must struggle with the problem of conferring a sacred status upon objects pre-dominantly classified as profane.'[19] Perhaps earth concerned people of other faiths can assist us in this struggle. Inter-religious relations – and religion itself – were skirted in the UNED (UK) meetings I attended previous to, and after, the unsuccessful Johannesburg Earth Summit. There can be no global 'sustainable development' which excludes justice to indigenous people, including Arab Moslems and Christians suffering ethnic cleansing by the State of Israel, no sustainable sufficiency, no health of the planetary biosphere, as we have known it, without inter-religious endeavour. In one of the richest ecological texts in the New Testament, the Lucan Jesus, as a reader in his native Nazareth synagogue, points in that direction.

Conclusion

We encounter Jesus at Nazareth, in his 'own country', with our whole person, including our imaginative power. Remember Newman, 'It is the concrete being that reasons, the whole man moves.' Confronted with mounting evidence of climatic disruption and earth deterioration in all its living and non-living components, I am more convinced than I was as a young scholastic on retreats that directors who committed full days to contemplation of Jesus in his Nazareth years were wise. On the surface of the early testimony, there appears little we can know, or contemplate, concerning Jesus in his formative Nazareth years, little about Jesus and the Nazareth soil community we can discover. But beneath the surface, with imagination's 'auxiliar light', we can recover, and discover, a lot. In this chapter, like those retreat days 'at' Nazareth, I suggest that we contemplate Jesus with the Nazareth natural world, and that we do so close to nature ourselves. Even if our own natural 'world' is a carefully tidied retreat house garden, like Detroit's Manresa on its river, or Ireland's Manresa, at Dundalk, or if our 'nature' is an urban park, or our own back garden or, as it is for all, sooner or later, a window box, or a bird feeder, there we can revisit Jesus, at

Nazareth, often. Pray with, and to, him there, where he spent most of his earthly life, working with wood, and in family fields, with special family olives and vines, with compost, cisterns, heirloom seeds, and stock, with much loved sheep and goats, the family donkey, a rooster, and hens with chicks beneath their wings. Communicate with him beyond the village, in the midst of lower Galilee, with the foxes, raptors, birds, insects, and wild flowers with which he shared and loved the hills. Nazareth especially empowers us to see, in St Ninian's words, Jesus 'reflected in every plant and insect, every bird and animal and man and woman'.

Consider, with sympathy, too, the wrench it must have been for Jesus to leave parents, siblings, and neighbours – and his special animals with which he had lived, and worked, and shared, and communicated. Consider the almost unexpected wound in leaving the fruit with which a gardener has a near personal relationship, and the fertile soil he had dug and weeded, irrigated, fed, and maintained. Young men leave home because they have a job to do, a mission to fulfil, a rainbow to pursue. Jesus left all this, for all that. His purpose was to preach God's kingdom, within which he already realised he had an important part, and if necessary, to suffer, even die, to inaugurate that kingdom, to reconcile all things to God, the Father to whom he prayed as 'Abba'. That kingdom, on earth as in heaven, and that reconciliation include, and some of us will think especially include, the soil community of which he himself was a part, in Nazareth of Galilee from which, thought Nathanael, good things cannot come.

Notes:
1. Olivier Clement, The Roots of Christian Mysticism (London: New City, 1993), p. 223.
2. Eusebius, The History of the Church from Christ to Constantine, 1, 7.14, trans., G. A. Williamson (Harmondsworth: Penguin, 1965), p. 55.
3. Raymond E. Brown, The Birth of the Messiah (London: Geoffrey Chapman, 1993), p. 209.

4. Craig A. Evans, 'Context, Family, and Formation', in *The Cambridge Companion to Jesus,* Markus Bockmuehl, ed. (Cambridge: CUP, 2001), p. 14.
5. John P. Meier, *A Marginal Jew, Rethinking the Historical Jesus,* Vol. 1 (New York: Doubleday, 1991), p. 311.
6. Edward P. Echlin, 'Jesus and the Earth Community', *EcoTheology,* 2 (January 1997), pp. 31-47.
7. Meier, *A Marginal Jew,* Vol I, p. 308.
8. Harry Gamble, *Books and Readers in the Early Church* (New Haven: Yale University Press, 1995), pp. 5-8.
9. Josephus, *The Jewish War* (Harmondsworth: Penguin Books, 1981), p. 192.
10. Ibid., p. 211.
11. Meier, *A Marginal Jew,* Vol. I, p. 279.
12. Jeremy Slane, 'A Layman's Guide to Figs', *Fruit News, the Magazine of the Friends of Brogdale* (Winter 2001-2002), pp. 8-9.
13. Josephus, *Jewish War,* p. 128.
14. Eusebius, *History of the Church,* 3, 20.1, p. 126.
15. C. H. Dodd, *The Founder of Christianity* (London: Fontana, 1978), p. 50.
16. N. T. Wright, *Jesus and the Victory of God* (London: SPCK, 1996), p. 536.
17. McKibben, *The Comforting Whirlwind,* p. 52.
18. Wright, *Jesus and the Victory of God,* p. 295.
19. Paul B. Thompson, *The Spirit of the Soil, Agriculture and Environmental Ethics* (London: Routledge, 1995), p. 9.

CHAPTER FOUR

The Cosmic Jordan

The entire nature of the waters perceived that you had visited
them – seas, deeps, rivers, springs and pools all thronged
together to receive the blessing from your footsteps.
(Jacob of Sarugh)

Christ is never without water.
(Tertullian)

Growing up in a state grasped on three sides by the Great Lakes,
with myriad smaller lakes, rivers, and streams, in both upper
and lower peninsulas, I took abundant fresh water for granted.
Even during the war, when precious commodities were rationed,
water flowed freely in the living rivers and lakes, dropping as
gentle rain and, in winter, snow, from heaven. Some neighbours
kept boats on nearby rivers and lakes. My uncle kept a cabin
cruiser, which resembles a caravan on water, on nearby Lake St
Clair, which he shared with my father for fishing trips into
Canadian waters where people were fewer and fish teeming. At
our first cottage, on Lake Huron, we enjoyed mains electricity
but no mains water. We did not need it. We had a well with
abundant potable water, a chestnut rain barrel, and a pump
house, from which pipes ran out into the lake to supply more
water in summer. My father connected the long lead pipes in
spring, laying them on the rocky bottom of the lake for a few
hundred metres and then, in autumn, disconnecting them and
bringing them in before autumn frosts and winter ice. The theory
then (which would soon change) was that if you drew water far
enough from shore, it was safe to drink without boiling! Where
wooded springs and rivers were remote from settlements, it was
considered safe to drink from them too. In the Scouts I learned to
take river water from below a rapids, which supposedly
cleansed it from impurities. So we would lie face downwards

and gulp river water downstream from a rushing rapids, often
startling a trout or small egg-sized turtle, with which the rivers
abounded, as our heads invaded their domain. Everywhere in
Michigan, in both peninsulas, there were clear lakes of various
sizes, shapes, and biodiversities.

After some summers on Lake Huron, and a few more on
Lake Erie, I was sent to a boys' camp, in the north woods, called
'Skegemog'. Camp Skegemog nestled among the birch and pine
of Skegemog Point, a narrow promontory of land resting like a
finger between two lakes, Elk and Round. Hence the beautiful
Native American word 'Skegemog', for 'meeting of the waters'.
Elk Lake was larger, rougher, and deeper than Round, and not
without hazards. So we swam, boated, fished, paddled canoes,
and had our campfires on Round Lake, with counsellors never
far away. Occasionally, on settled and still days, we were permitted to row around the sandy, pebbled Skegemog Point into
Elk Lake, where the fishing was better. There was a chapel, in
traditional frontier log cabin style, near the tip of the Point,
where the Elk and Round waters met. Life began in, and with,
water, and cannot continue without it. Skegemog Point was a
well chosen place for worship. I wondered if the Indians, as we
called the indigenous peoples who preceded us in the woods
and on the lakes, and who left us with so many of their mellifluous words, such as Skegemog, Muskegon, and (for a waterfall)
Tequamenon, had prayed in their strange-seeming ways at that
same spot. Did they find their Father, and Maker, in those same
pines and waters? I suspect they did. Certainly they lived more
gently and sustainably with God's waters than did the trappers
and settlers and suburbanites. We were fortunate to have a
young priest chaplain, Frank McPhillips, whose homilies at
Sunday eucharists raised some of these same questions, and
kept our attention. Fr McPhillips didn't leave his sermons behind in the chapel either, but questioned us about them when he
met us during the week, and gave small prizes for alert answers.
He also accustomed us to the Sacrament of Reconciliation, or
Penance as we then called the practice of confessing our failings

to God and the church, receiving absolution from a priest con-
fessor. So on Saturday evenings, as the fireflies flickered over the
waters like moving candles, and the crickets and Round Lake
frogs sang in polyphony around the chapel, we mentioned our
faults of the week, if we wished, to Fr McPhillips. I don't recall
Frank McPhillips, or any adult, teaching us that earth abuse was
a sin, although my father and uncles, the writings of John Muir,
and the teaching of the Bible taught respect for the earth, and
said it was wrong to hurt it. We are more conscious now that it is
wrong to abuse the earth – and the future. As Orthodox Bishop
John of Pergamon says, 'to hurt the earth is a sin'.

To call Michigan the 'water wonderland', as fledgling tourist
boards did, though partisan, was not exaggerated. At least not
then. We had plenty of snow, which kept the woods and fields
both warm and permeable. In winter, 'the January thaw' fed the
rivers, which in turn fed the lakes. In spring came Al Jolson's
'April Showers'. The thought of water scarcity, except perhaps
in the Mojave desert or in the world of Beau Geste and the
Foreign Legion, was simply unimaginable. Recent United
Nations reports estimate over two billion people short of drinking and sanitation water, and two million children unwell from
water related illnesses. Unless we radically change our fossil
fuel consumption, these figures will increase. Climatologists estimate that, with human induced climatic disruptions, or global
warming as it is misleadingly called, the Great Lakes may sink
as much as four feet. Even now, lake water is evaporating in
winter as in summer; in winter the lakes are not freezing as they
did. Here in southern England, I garden organically, through
winter floods and storms, summer droughts, hosepipe bans,
and with a pond and two water butts that, in droughts, empty
all too quickly. Conservation biologists warn about mercury fill-
ings, shampoos, detergents, paint and varnish, pesticides, mo-
torway and runway runoff, and pharmaceuticals, including
gender bending substances especially hazardous to children,
pouring into landfill and aquifers, contaminating drinking
water. During the 2002 Johannesburg Summit, the 2003 Year of

Fresh Water, and regularly since, climatologists have warned of water stress and shortages, even in southern England. Indeed overcrowded England is the most water stressed and water short nation in the EU. Hydrologists estimate that over half of the earth's rivers are seriously depleted, and that nearly the same percentage of earth's people are seriously short of fresh water.

I am convinced that the Christian churches, the Jesus movement which, in Jesus risen, exists everywhere on earth, have considerably more than has been realised to offer the earth community in our tradition of love of water. Water is included among the creatures reconciled in Jesus, it is within the new creation. Water is the source of life, which flowed from the side of Christ, the New Adam, onto the renewed earth, in the presence of the New Eve, and the disciple representing ourselves (Jn 19:34). Christians are water people. As Tertullian, the third-century North African lawyer said succinctly, 'Christ is never without water' (*On Baptism*, 9.3). Where the Jesus people are, there is, or should be, Skegemog – the meeting of the waters.

To the Jordan
More even than Elk and Round Lakes, the Jordan is Christian water. After leaving Nazareth, where he had family, and was an accepted craftsman, Jesus dwelt for a while in the Judean wilderness, in the circle of John the Baptist. John is an important person, forever associated with the river. Of John, biblical scholar G. R. Beasley Murray says, 'John the Baptist forms the bridgehead between the old order and the new, not in such a fashion as to belong to neither, but in such a fashion as to belong to both.'[1] How Jesus heard of John, where they met (Luke says they met when Jesus was in the womb!), how long Jesus remained with John, and whether John was Jesus' 'mentor', we do not know. Jesus' weeks or months with John, in the Judean wilderness, and in the southern Jordan rift, integrate the mighty river, the wilderness, and wilderness fare and attire, within salvation history and salvation ecology.

The gospels agree that John preached imminent judgement, baptised in the river, and moved around the wilderness, preaching and baptising on both banks of the Jordan. Mark and Matthew say that he wore a camel's hair garment, with a leather belt, similar to the rough garb of the great – and awaited – prophet Elijah (2 Kgs 1:8). John's rough clothing resembles Bedouin attire. We do not know whether Jesus wore Bedouin clothes while in the desert, or the similar protective clothes he wore at Nazareth. Theological art, and our imaginations, picture him both ways. John also ate Bedouin fare, including locusts, or grasshoppers, and wild honey. This again attests to John's wilderness and ascetic lifestyle, at least when he and his followers lived in the dry desert. Even in recent years, during recurrent food shortages, Palestinians, especially near the Jordan or during Israeli incursions, and inhabitants of Ethiopia and the Arabian desert have eaten locusts, grass, and other free food. The Baptist's 'wild honey' could have been bee honey, or secretions from desert trees. The Essenes, on the northern corner of the Dead Sea, kept bees. Like the Bedouins, John and his group possibly kept grazing stock, which supplied some milk and its derivatives. And they may have cultivated plots in oases. In any scenario, Jesus, in his weeks or months with the Baptist's community, would have experienced a wilderness lifestyle. John was no 'pillar ascetic', but a mobile preacher, baptising at Bethany and at Aenon, probably near fords, where travellers crossed and where immersion was possible.

The Jordan wilderness teems with wildlife. Even now, despite our addiction to agribusiness which decimates birds and, especially in Mediterranean countries, the deadly sport of wild bird shooting, an estimated 500 million birds, representing 500 species, still fly above the Jordan twice annually. Migrating birds and wild animals demonstrate the connectedness and interdependence of the wildlife habitats of the earth. The Jordan migrants are special, for they fly above the footsteps of Jesus in the wilderness; like human pilgrims visiting and being baptised in the river below, they, the river itself, and all earth's creatures are reconciled in Jesus' baptism, which is related to his passion. 'Jesus Christ, not with the water only, but with the water and the blood' (1 Jn 5:6). Gregory of Nyssa, a fourth-century Cappadocian bishop and theologian, notes, as do many Eastern writers, and we ourselves in our imagination, that the Jordan receives the first fruits of cosmic redemption: 'The Jordan alone among all rivers has received the first fruits of sanctification and blessing.'[2]

Jesus is Baptised

During a quarterly theology evening in our house, a retired clergyman said he found Jesus' baptism embarrassing, because Jesus was sinless and baptism is associated with the forgiveness of sins. He expressed, with candour, a recurrent feeling of many people within the Jesus movement. We need to remind ourselves, and those we teach, that Jesus submitted to John's baptism, not for forgiveness of personal sins, but in solidarity with a fickle Israel that did need repentance and forgiveness before the imminent judgement. Jesus sought forgiveness with and within the lost sheep of the house of Israel. In his baptism Jesus acknowledges human relatedness. He was, and is, related to his fellow Jews, to all humanity, and to all water and earth creatures. Because in his humanity Jesus is a microcosm of material creation, including ourselves, we are washed by the Jordan in his baptism. The fourth-century theologian and bishop, Athanasius, wrote, 'When the Lord, as man, was washed in the Jordan, it was we who were washed in him and by him' (*Against the Arians*, 1.47). Nor should we wonder that Jesus *learned*, especially wilderness lore, from the Baptist, and that he was tempted, in the wilderness. We profess in our creeds that Jesus was human, like us in all save sin. If Jesus never learned and if he were never tempted, he would not be the incarnate Jesus of our creeds, the microcosm of our universe, whom we long to know, love, and follow. Donald Senior, an American biblical scholar, writes, 'Jesus did not go through the motions of being human. He was human. He had to learn, to search, to be a fellow traveller in the sometimes tortuous pilgrimage of human existence.'[3] At his baptism, Jesus may have recognised his special, even unique, importance in God's kingdom. Durham University's David Brown is one of many theologians who think Jesus had a mystical experience at the Jordan: 'In all probability, the baptism of Jesus by John did mark the inauguration of his ministry, and from that point on he had a firm conviction of the very special role to which he was called, in part perhaps based upon some visionary or mystical experience he had at the time.'[4]

Mark's gospel hesitates not at all to say that Jesus was baptised by John. Indeed, he begins his gospel not at the birth of Jesus, but at his baptism: 'In those days Jesus came from Nazareth of Galilee and was baptised by John in the Jordan' (Mk 1:9). John's baptism was probably by complete immersion. For Mark it was also an epiphany: the heavens broke open, the Spirit descended and remained on Jesus, and a heavenly voice said, 'You are my beloved Son, with thee I am well pleased' (Mk 1:11). The Spirit over the waters recalls the first creation. At Jesus' baptism new creation has begun. The Father's words echo Psalm 2:7, a royal psalm. The association of Jesus with kingship recurs throughout the gospels. This is ecologically significant because, in Jewish hopes, good kings ensure good weather, ample rain, and fertile soil (Ps 72:3, 6, 16). The Jordan epiphany, or revelation of Jesus' identity, also recalls the peaceable kingdom, wherein the Spirit rests upon the ruler in the midst of harmonious creation (Is 11:6-9; Ps 72:9). Once again we notice Jesus, Saviour and King, in the midst of earth creatures. The Jordan revelation, say Orthodox Christians, surpasses the Magi's, for at the Jordan there is an epiphany of all three Divine Persons.

After Mark's terse riverine scene, when reading Matthew we find ourselves on familiar ground, or perhaps better, at a familiar ford of a much loved river. Matthew adds some leisurely brush strokes to Mark's typically hurried picture. John still wears rough Bedouin garb, and eats wilderness fare, but there are more ecological metaphors in his preaching, some of them almost shocking to anyone unaccustomed to wilderness prophets. He castigates the Jewish leaders as a 'brood of vipers', an uncomplimentary comparison with the ubiquitous much feared reptile which gives birth to frightening, living progeny, for which we may have pity. He points to rocks, which are even more common than vipers, saying that God could raise up children of Abraham from desert rocks. He compares the Jewish leaders to diseased fruit trees, the only ones that could be felled; even now the axe is at their roots. In another metaphor, drawn from grain harvest, he compares the coming judgement to a winnowing, which separates grain from chaff. Chaff, like diseased wood, was still good, but for fuel or compost. In Matthew's baptism scene, John hesitates to baptise Jesus. 'I need to be baptised by you, and do you come to me?' (Mt 3:14). Matthew, like Mark, describes the epiphany: the heavens break open, the Father's voice is heard, this time by all present, and the Spirit descends as a dove upon Jesus – the second, or new creation – in a scene that will be represented in Christian art for over two millennia, beginning in the early catacombs (Mt 3:17).

In Luke, as in Matthew, the Baptist employs wilderness metaphors: the viper's brood, good and bad fruit trees, the axe at the root of unproductive trees, the endless desert stones. Luke, however, does not describe Jesus' baptism. The epiphany occurs after Jesus has been baptised, off-stage, as it were. Luke leaves no doubt as to which of the prophets is greater. When they first met, John leapt in his mother's womb, and Elizabeth deferred to Mary (Lk 1:42-44). Similarly, in the fourth gospel, the Baptist himself leaves no doubt as to who is supreme: 'John bore witness to him, and cried, "This was he of whom I said, 'He who comes after me ranks before me, for he was before me'."' (Jn 1:15).

In Jesus, 'the first born' of creation, God's Word enters our earth community as a human being. In becoming flesh, Jesus unites himself to all people and to all earth creatures. Pope John Paul II includes the cosmic dimension of the incarnation when he writes, '"The first born of all creation", becoming incarnate in the individual humanity of Christ, unites himself in some way

with the entire reality of man, which is also "flesh" … and in this
reality with all "flesh", with the whole creation' (*Dom. et Viv.*
50.3). In Jesus the whole earth community is reconciled to God,
and transformed. Cardinal Avery Dulles observes, 'To merit the
significance Christian faith attributes to it, the incarnation of the
Word must have a bearing not only on human destiny but on
that of the larger universe of nature … The Word of God, in as-
suming a full human existence, entered into a kind of union with
the cosmos.'[5] The whole earth community, therefore, which God
enters in the flesh of Jesus, is reconciled to God and transformed.
When Jesus enters the Jordan, the waters and creatures dependent on water, are sanctified by the presence of God's Word
made flesh. All waters are connected – water is like the blood of
the earth. All waters are the cosmic Jordan. All waters are
Jordanised, sanctified, recreated, when the Spirit again moves
over the waters at Jesus' baptism. A second-century Syrian ode
says beautifully:

> The dove fluttered over the head of our Lord, the Saviour,
> Because he was her head.[6]

Jesus Never Without Water
Although the early Christians remembered Jesus primarily as an
itinerant preacher and teacher, he may also have baptised
throughout his ministry (Jn 1:31). Some even confused him with
the famous Jordan baptiser: '"Who do men say that I am?" And
they told him, "Some say John the Baptist. Others, Elijah, or one
of the prophets".' (Mk 8:28). Especially in John's gospel, Jesus is
near water all his life. The Spirit descends and remains upon
him in new creation at the Jordan. He calls disciples at the lake.
At his first 'sign', the miracle at Cana, water saw its Master's face
– and blushed. To Nicodemus, he explains that a person is re-
born through water and the Spirit. To a Samaritan woman at
Jacob's well, Jesus compares himself to fresh, living water,
which, unlike cistern water, rushes with life: 'Whoever drinks of
the water that I shall give him will never thirst; the water that I
shall give him will become in him a spring of water welling up

to eternal life' (Jn 4:13-14). At Jerusalem he cures a man at Bethesda pool, heals a man born blind, using spittle and sending him to the pool of Siloam. At the Last Supper Jesus washes his disciples' feet (Jn 13:14). From his open side, on the cross, there flows blood and water. The final pages of the Bible, in the Book of Revelation, say that in the new creation water will flow from the throne of Jesus, the Lamb (Rev 22:1). To repeat Tertullian's words, with which we began this chapter, 'Christ is never without water.' Redemption in Jesus reaches every particle, every pore, of the earth which, like our bodies, and the soil in which our plants grow, and the fruit of plants, the soil which animals inhabit, and their bodies, is 'virtual water'. Of the whole earth community redeemed in Jesus, Jeremiah's evocative words are true: 'Their life shall become like a watered garden' (Jer 31:12).

With the Wild Animals
When Jesus left the Baptist's circle, the gospels say he remained for a while in the wilderness where he pondered his future and was tempted. Mark adds that 'he was with the wild animals, and the angels ministered to him' (Mk 1:13). Although Mark, characteristically, gives no further details, in his gospel 'to be with' means solidarity and fellowship. Theological poets, artists, and some theologians detect intimations of the peaceable kingdom in Mark's few, tantalising words. Stanley Spencer, in a painting now at Perth, Australia, portrays Jesus as a stout peasant, gently cradling a scorpion on his hand. Robert Graves, touchingly, suggests that a 'poor innocent' scapegoat may have attached himself to his Master in the wilderness:

Followed in Jesus' ways,
Sure guard behind him kept,
Tears like a lover wept.
(Robert Graves, *In the Wilderness*)

When we contemplate Mark's few words about Jesus with the wilderness animals, we discover the new Adam, and Prince of Peace, with his sensate creatures. Mark's picture reminds us that the desert is a place of life. There are life-giving springs even in

deserts. Dew, condensation, and succulent plants provide moisture. Wadis and almost hidden springs enable biodiversity. Life
thrives in oases where there is living water. Water enables, and
preserves, life in the desert, as it does in our gardens, orchards,
and fields. 'The thing that makes a desert beautiful', said St
Exupery, 'is that somewhere it hides a well.'

The Cosmic Jordan

In early Christian centuries, Jesus' baptism in the Jordan and
Easter complemented each other, as important liturgical feasts.
Both celebrate the sanctification of the whole earth, including
the earth's waters. In both feasts, Jesus 'crosses' the Jordan, entering the new creation. In his entering the river, his baptism,
epiphany, and anointing by the Spirit, Jesus sanctifies all waters,
setting them 'afire'. Justin, a second-century apologist and martyr, says, 'When Jesus had gone to the river Jordan, where John
was baptising, and when he had stepped into the water, a fire
was kindled in the Jordan.'[7] In Holy Week, we recall Jesus' descent into the fiery Jordan, and his sanctification of the waters,
when we immerse the paschal candle in water. Jesus' baptism
demonstrates that the incarnation and redemption in Jesus, who
in his humanity is a microcosm of the earth, includes the whole
earth community. Neither the Baptist nor Jesus invented water
baptism. Ancient peoples, including the contemporary Essenes
of the Dead Sea, practised ritual lustrations. John and Jesus,
however, radically reinterpreted their washings. Through his
own descent into the Jordan and his baptism by John, and later
by baptising others, Jesus gave a new dignity to the Jordan and
through that river to all the waters of the earth. All waters are
now the cosmic Jordan sanctified by Jesus' presence. At the
Jordan Jesus gave John's baptism a new content. Jesus' baptism
– and baptising – is the institution or beginning of our own, in
which we receive God's Spirit. Kilian McDonnell writes:

> No one suggests that Jesus invented baptism. Rather the con-
> tention is that he more radically reinterpreted the going
> down into the waters than John the Baptist interpreted the

many water baths in the history of Israel. The baptism to be found in the Christian community is indeed John's baptism, but given new content and a new teleology, in fact, completely changed and transformed. The new content is a new mode of God's presence as expressed in the voice of the Father and the descent of the Spirit in the form of the dove, a participation in the giving of the Spirit to Jesus without measure.[8]

The church has never forgotten the cosmic, ecological significance of baptism. A catechism issued after the sixteenth-century Council of Trent, for example, describes Jesus' baptism as the 'institution' of our own, and the sanctification, or empowerment, of water: 'This sacrament was instituted by our Lord when, having been baptised by John, he gave to water the power of sanctifying.'[9] More recently, the Catechism of the Catholic Church, issued in 1994, after the Second Vatican Council (1962-65), relates the Spirit moving over the waters at the first creation to the baptism of Jesus, the prelude to the new creation: 'The Spirit who had hovered over the waters of the first creation descended then on the Christ as a prelude of the new creation, and the Father revealed Jesus as his beloved Son.'[10]

At beautiful Mount Hermon, where the mighty river gathers, the sources appear mysteriously hidden, subterranean. Once formed, the river widens gradually, only to disappear into the blue Sea of Galilee, then to reappear and continue south, until it finally vanishes, again almost mysteriously, into the Dead Sea. These striking features of the sacred river elicit symbolism. Inspired by its mysterious origins, and its final disappearance, Eastern writers say the river flows 'from paradise to paradise'. Its waters engender new creation. Jesus' baptism not only sanctifies the living river, but makes the river the cosmic Jordan, affecting all the waters of the world. A Byzantine blessing of waters prays:

> For the sanctification of these waters by the indwelling and power of the Holy Spirit, let us pray.
> That the Lord may send upon them the grace of redemption, the blessing of Jordan, let us beseech the Lord.

That they may be blessed as were Jordan's waves, let us be-
seech the Lord.[11]

Coptic and Armenian Christians call the baptismal font 'the
Jordan'. In the words of an Armenian rite, 'The deacon leads
him that is to be baptised from the west and brings him to the
east over against the Jordan [the font], to the left hand of the
priest … and after he has baptised all the children, he shall pour
water over his hands in the Jordan, and shall wash the surroundings of the Jordan and the cross.'[12] All the world's waters,
including inland rivers, and lakes like those at Skegemog in
Michigan, are blessed by Jesus' footsteps. Jacob of Sarugh, a
Syrian Christian, wrote, in the sixth century, 'The entire nature
of the waters perceived that you had visited them – seas, deeps,
rivers, springs and pools all thronged together to receive the
blessing from your footsteps.'[13] In our own time, Francis
Thompson, grasping the cosmic presence of Christ and of the
Jordan, wrote:

Yea, in the night, my Soul, my daughter,
Cry, – clinging Heaven by the hems;
And lo, Christ walking on the water
Not of Gennesareth but Thames!
(Francis Thompson, *The Kingdom of God*)

Spring is the season especially evocative of new creation, when
the biosphere shines and bursts with new life. Spring is the season of Jesus' resurrection, the beginning of the new creation
wherein we, followers of Jesus the new Adam, become his
image (1 Cor 15:42-49). At spring we bless baptismal water, we
baptise new Christians, and renew our own. For baptism too is a
new creation. Jean Danielou writes:

The spring, the season in which God created the world, is an
annual anniversary of creation; that the resurrection of Christ
took place in the springtime indicates that it is also a new
creation. And baptism is, in turn, a new creation also. Thus, it
is not only the liturgical text that connects baptism with the
spring, the season setting itself is also found to be charged
with symbolic significance.[14]

In the early Christian centuries, some Christians delayed their baptisms, hoping to travel to Jesus' own river, to be baptised in spring in the Jordan where Jesus himself had been baptised. A famous delayer is Constantine the Great. When terminal illness struck suddenly in 337, the Emperor reluctantly requested baptism by Eusebius of Nicomedia, in the imperial city. Constantine said, 'I had thought to receive it in the waters of the Jordan ... but it pleases God, who knows what is best for us, that I should receive it here. So be it, then, and without delay.'[15] Constantine realised that all water is the cosmic Jordan. As Tertullian wrote graphically in the third century, 'It makes no difference whether a man be washed in a sea or a pool, a stream or a fount, a lake or a trough; nor is there any distinction between those whom John baptised in the Jordan and those whom Peter baptised in the Tiber.'[16]

Recognising the sanctification of all waters by Jesus' baptism, and passion, Orthodox Christians bless seas, rivers, and lakes, especially at the 'Epiphany' feast commemorating Jesus' baptism. They place the cross in seas, lakes, and rivers. Orthodox, like many Irish, Christians, do not pour consecrated water into drains, but onto plants and the soil, or as John Anthony McGuckin notes, the water is drunk respectfully, as is consecrated wine after Catholic eucharists. Echoes of this respect for water, sanctified by Jesus' baptism, appears in an Armenian hymn quoted by Vigen Guroian, an Armenian theologian and gardener:

Christ is baptised, and all creatures are hallowed.

Grant then to us remission of sins,

hallowing us anew with water and spirit.[17]

Nor is respect for water confined to Orthodoxy and the Celtic fringe. The Men of Kent, and Kentish Men, sponsor an annual sea blessing, on the feast of St James, the patron of oystermen, at Whitstable. At the Ravenna baptisteries, both Arian and Orthodox mosaics picture the Hellenic nature god worshipping Jesus in the Jordan. Other medieval art, as in the eleventh-century Daphne baptismal mosaic, portrays the supplanted nature god

fleeing the scene. In still another portrayal, a fifteenth-century
Armenian Bible depicts the Baptist and his followers, the riverine flora, and fish of the river, all bowing to Jesus, the One who
is, and was, 'before' John, while the Spirit, as a dove, descends
upon him. Beneath 'the unoffending feet', the water monster lies
vanquished, echoing God's words to Adam departing Paradise,
that a descendant of the woman will crush the monster's head
(Gen 3:15). Of this hapless creature, Bishop Cyril of Jerusalem
wrote in the fourth century, 'Since he was destined to crush the
serpent's head, Jesus went down into the water and bound the
strong one, so that we might receive "power to tread on snakes
and scorpions". (Lk 10:19). It was no small beast, but a fearful
one.'[18]

Conclusion: from the Jordan to Globalisation

We now realise that, through evaporation, precipitation, wind,
clouds, and birds, all waters are interrelated, all are the Jordan –
and the Nile, Tigris, Thames, Ganges, Shannon, and Mississippi.
In recognising Jesus' impact on all water, Jacob of Sarugh anticipated modern hydrology: 'The entire nature of the waters perceived that you had visited them.'[19]

In temperate zones, soil, permeated by water, is held together
by water so that soil, and the fruits of soil, are 'virtual water'.
Rain, mists, and dew infiltrate the soil. Trees and plants and animals drink from aquifers, and transpire water. When through
deforestation, intensive farming, unsustainable construction,
and climate change, soil is covered, dried, and desiccated, it
ceases to be 'virtual water', and erodes into seas and rivers or
into the atmosphere as dust. Even today, centuries after bronze
age people stripped Mediterranean slopes of trees, the 'wine
clear' Mediterranean turns brown in winter, where rain washes
remaining soil into the sea. To export avocados, bananas, and
citrus, from irrigated plantations, is to export virtual water, to
import fruit and vegetables is to import water. Rome imported
virtual water, and soil fertility, from Sicily and Carthage, in the
form of grain. Water contributed to the Punic wars – and the

deletion of Carthage. The Galilee, and Judea, of Jesus, through winter harvesting of rain, was self-sufficient in food and water. Today's Israel, overdeveloped and wasteful of water, imports food – and therefore virtual water.

Jesus' baptism in the Jordan invites Christian respect, even reverence, for water. David Toolan SJ, of *America* and *Spirit-Earth*, writes, 'Our duty is to collaborate with God in making signs that give grace – to make a sacrament of the earth.'[20] When we demonstrate our reverence and love of the earth, and the water which circulates everywhere on earth, because the earth is included in redemption in Jesus, we sacramentalise the earth, signifying his presence. By using, with reverence and restraint, whenever possible local food and drink, and reducing imports, we enable other people to preserve their local water. By reducing air travel, and food miles, we reduce emissions which damage climate – and, therefore, water. By harvesting some rain water, for our gardens, ponds, and plants, we conserve in a small way our region's water, allowing people already short of water to conserve their own.

Restraint towards importation of 'virtual water' in food and drink counters the tenacious earth destructive 'infinite resource illusion' which infects, and could ultimately destroy, America. Thirsty Palestinian Arabs and African peasants struggle to survive on fewer than 30 litres of water per day. In Britain, people consume about 135 litres a day. In Las Vegas, people consume an estimated 1500 litres per day.[21] John Carroll, Conservation Professor at New Hampshire University, frankly regrets 'a consumptive lifestyle that knows no limit (and refuses to consider any concept of limits), a lifestyle predicated on growth for its own sake (the disease of growthism, which is what unrestrained capitalism is all about).'[22] Great Britain, despite one of the densest populations on earth, is also reluctant to consider limits. Since 1945 much of the island's best agricultural land, rich in fertility and virtual water, has been taken out of agriculture. An estimated – and staggering – 80 per cent of this fallow land has been covered with housing – and, as family disintegration, migrations, unsustainable procreation, and buying on credit continue, demand for more housing – and roads and runways – on arable land persists.[23]

Calculated dependence on fossil fuel transport for imported food and medicines, especially in islands such as Malta, Ireland, and Britain, is an inevitable, self-induced tragedy that soon will happen. Every bioregion, no matter how 'growing' its 'economy', needs sufficient soil and water to feed people, animals, and plants, in at least partial self-sufficiency, without dependence on fossil fuel driven imports. One of the paramount services Christians in developed regions can do for people everywhere is to promote local, at least partial, self-sufficiency in food and drink, and independence of foreign 'trade' for decent survival. What the vast majority of politicians, journalists, economists, and developers find enormously inconvenient to realise is that every field, brown or green, is precious, fragile, necessary, irreplaceable for a bioregion's continuance, and that all soil, all fields, and not just 'SSSIs' and 'greenbelts', are virtual water. Appreciation of the cosmic Jordan motivates Christians to live locally and sustainably, correcting what Professor Carroll calls 'economic growthism', and the insidious infinite resource illusion. Commitment to Jesus, Lord of the soil and water, inspires us to accept the limitations under which life on this redeemed planet is granted.

The deep, imaginative Christian tradition expresses, in theological art and poetry, Jesus in the Jordan vanquishing, or welcoming, the resident nature gods. In his ministry Jesus touched, and healed, whole persons in their bodily existence. Significantly, for us who exist 'to make a sacrament of the earth', our baptismal services retain rites of exorcism. There may be timely value in exorcisms of the demons which encourage earth abuse, over-construction, over-population, economic growthism, climate damage, and unsustainable consumption. The *Catechism of the Catholic Church* contains an interesting paragraph, which we may ponder:

Since Baptism signifies liberation from sin and from its

instigator the devil, one or more exorcisms are pronounced over the candidate. The celebrant then anoints him with the oil of catechumens, or lays his hands on him, and he explicitly renounces Satan. Thus prepared, he is able to confess the faith of the church, to which he will be 'entrusted' by baptism.[24]

The 'faith of the church' with which baptised Christians are entrusted includes appreciation of the world's waters, and the virtual water of the soil, because, in Jesus, God descended into the living Jordan, setting the waters afire.

Notes:
1. G. R. Beasley Murray, *Jesus and the Kingdom of God* (Grand Rapids: Eerdmanns, 1986), p. 94.
2. Gregory of Nyssa, 'On the Baptism of Christ', PG 46:593. Cf. Kilian McDonnell, *The Baptism of Jesus in the Jordan, the Trinitarian and Cosmic Order of Salvation* (Collegeville: Liturgical Press, 1996), pp. 75-76.
3. Donald Senior, *Jesus: A Gospel Portrait* (New Jersey: Paulist Press, 1992), p. 78.
4. David Brown, *Tradition and Imagination, Revelation and Change* (Oxford: Oxford University Press, 1999), p. 282.
5. Avery Dulles, *The Catholicity of the Church* (Oxford: Clarendon Press, 1985), pp. 34-35.
6. *The Odes of Solomon: The Syriac Texts*, J. H. Charlesworth, ed. (Missoula: Scholars Press, 1977), p. 98.
7. Justin Martyr, 'Dialogue With Trypho', *The Ante-Nicene Fathers, Vol. I. The Apostolic Fathers, Justin Martyr, and Irenaeus*, A. Cleveland Coxe, ed. (Edinburgh: T. & T. Clark, 1993), p. 243.
8. McDonnell, *The Baptism of Jesus*, p. 172.
9. *Catechism of the Council of Trent*, J. A. McHugh, & C. J. Callan, eds. (New York: Wagner, 1934), p. 170.
10. *Catechism of the Catholic Church* (London: Geoffrey Chapman, 1994), 1224, p. 279.
11. E. C. Whitaker, *Documents of the Baptismal Liturgy* (London: SPCK, 1970), p. 78.
12. Ibid., p. 95.
13. In McDonnell, *The Baptism of Jesus*, p. 61.
14. Danielou, *The Bible and the Liturgy*, p. 194.
15. John Julius Norwich, *Byzantium, The Early Centuries* (London: Penguin, 1990), p. 76.

16. Tertullian, 'On Baptism', *The Ante-Nicene Fathers, Vol. III, Tertullian*, Alexander Roberts, ed. (Edinburgh: T. &T. Clark, 1993), pp. 670-671.

17. Guroian, *Inheriting Paradise, Meditations on Gardening*, p. 86.

18. Catechetical Lecture 3, in *Cyril of Jerusalem*, Edward Yarnold SJ, ed. (London: Routledge, 2000), p. 94.

19. In McDonnell, *The Baptism of Jesus*, p. 61.

20. David Toolan SJ, 'Making Sacraments Out of Earth', *SpiritEarth* (February 2002), p. 2.

21. 'Water', *Church Times* (2 August 2002), pp. 13-20.

22. John Carroll, 'Sustainability and Spirituality', *SpiritEarth* (February 2002), p. 4.

23. Steve Connor, 'Way beyond bricks and mortar', Special Feature, *Green Futures* (June 2002), p. xiii.

24. *Catechism of the Catholic Church*, 1237, p. 281.

CHAPTER FIVE

Galilee to Jerusalem

On the mountain height of Israel will I plant it,
that it may bring forth boughs and bear fruit,
and become a noble cedar;
and under it will dwell all kinds of beast;
in the shade of its branches birds of every sort will nest.
(Ezek 17:23)

With what can we compare the kingdom of God,
or what parable shall we use for it?
It is like a grain of mustard seed,
which, when sown upon the ground,
is the smallest of all the seeds on earth;
yet when it is sown it grows up
and becomes the greatest of all shrubs,
and puts forth large branches,
so that the birds of the air can make nests in its shade.
(Mk 4:30-32)

Jesus' intimation, at the Jordan, of his life mission was not a 'once in a flash' event, like Hopkins' description of Paul's dramatic conversion. His gradual realisation of his importance in God's kingdom did not strike out of the Judean blue, but probably began in the long thoughts of youth, and in his prayers, in the Nazareth hills. The very fact that he chose to leave his village shows that, in his young manhood, God was guiding him.

Life-altering experiences, while not everyday occurrences, are not uncommon. I just mentioned Paul's. The persecutor became an apostle. Before Paul's persecution of Christians began, after Jesus' crucifixion and burial, two disciples who had known Jesus in his ministry experienced him risen, in a stranger who broke bread with them on the Emmaus road. Another famous change occurred in fourth-century Alexandria, when a young

Anthony pondered Jesus' words to the rich youth – and left all
to follow Jesus, as the first Christian solitary. Thomas Aquinas,
near the end of his life, had an experience that, he said, made all
his writings seem like straw. He wrote little thereafter. Ignatius
Loyola, resting at the Cardoner river 'which was running deep'
near Manresa, 'experienced a great clarity in his understanding,
such that in the whole course of his life, through sixty-two years,
even if he gathered up all the many helps he had had from God
and all the many things he knew and added them together, he
does not think they would amount to as much as he had received at that one time.'[1] Thereafter Ignatius never looked back.
These experiences – and few are out of the blue, like a lightening
crash – occur in less remarkable ways to the most ordinary pilgrims among us. When pondering my retirement ministry, after
I left regular lecturing, I reached an unassailable conviction
when gazing at and studying a medieval grange, built by the lay
brothers of Fountains Abbey. I realised that day that my 'third
age' vocation was to devote the rest of my life, with what education, training, and experience I had, to letting God's glory through
the earth, as a Christian environmentalist and ecological theologian. That expression, 'letting God's glory through' is from a
Gerard Manley Hopkins poem, 'The Blessed Virgin compared to
the Air we Breathe':

> who
> This one work has to do –
> Let all God's glory through,
> God's glory which would go
> Through her and from her flow
> Off, and no way but so.

We get a distantly analogous glimpse of Jesus' Jordan experience when we recall the experience of the Orkney poet, Edwin
Muir at an altar of the annunciation in Rome. Muir, a lifetime
Christian of the Book, later said, 'In Italy, I realised that God had
walked the earth.' At the Jordan, Jesus seems to have realised
something very similar, with the unique difference that God
who walked the earth was present in his own footsteps. We may

wonder if Jesus understood himself in the way an early
Christian hymn, used by Paul in a letter to Philippi, did – as one
'who humbled himself and became obedient unto death' (Phil
2:8). I think that, implicitly, he probably did. For he knew he
would encounter opposition, from Romans and fellow Jews, although he knew not what precise paths that enmity would take.
Jesus was also confident throughout his ministry that he would
be vindicated by God, as that early hymn also states. He knew,
from his attention to the Jewish writings, including Genesis,
Isaiah, and Ezekiel, and from the biodiverse voices of the
Nazareth and wilderness ecosystems, that all earth beings are
interdependent. He knew, at least implicitly, that other creatures
would share in his vindication, those 'in heaven, on earth, and
under the earth' (Phil 2:10).

The Earth as Grace

The living earth, where Jesus walked, reconciling to God all
earth creatures, is itself a grace, an amazing grace. Just to be
here, where Jesus walked on this rain watered planet, is a gratu-
itous gift of God. Through the incarnation, and embodied life of
Jesus, the earth is sanctified, filled with grace and deep glory.
The Jesus movement, the people we call the church, are earth
celebrators, with a mission to sacramentalise the earth, to let
God's glory through, as Mary did in her receptivity to the
incarnation and birth of Jesus. When we consider the creatures
with which we are especially entrusted, we can pray with the
psalmist, 'When thou sendest forth thy Spirit, they are created;
and thou renewest the face of the ground' (Ps 104:30). I keep
meeting people who discover Holy Mystery in 'their own' soil,
their gardens, their holdings, in their parks, in rivers and flowers and birds singing, in green life in cities, in all the poetry,
music, and beauty of the earth. Each of us who follows Jesus in
his ministry, all of us who together are the church, can let the
earth, especially where we live, be a sacrament of God's presence, his gift, his love for his creatures. When he stretches forth
his hands the special creatures around us are created, and recon-

ciled, and he renews the earth. Our mission and ministry is a
privileged one – to let all God's glory through.

Capernaum and the Sea
Cosmic redemption includes, in a special representative way,
the places on earth where Jesus lived and the creatures that he
knew. The flowers about which he spoke represent all flowers,
of all places and times. The domestic animals which accompanied him and bore his loads, represent all animals. As Joseph
Mary Plunkett wrote, 'His cross is every tree'. All flowers and
trees, all places and bioregions are interconnected with other
earth creatures, of all times and places. Jesus, embodied and embedded in his humanity, in his very presence within the earth
community reconciles all creatures, represented especially by
those he touched in Palestine. At the Jordan, assisted by the
imaginative gifts of theological artists, we glimpsed salvation
ecology represented in the nature gods, and the flora and fauna,
river and land animals, the Baptist and his followers, bowing in
praise towards Jesus, letting God's glory through. In this chapter we mention some of the special places and creatures Jesus
touched, in that brief span of his years here, which we call his
public ministry.

  After his brief stay in the wilderness, sorting out his relationships with the tempter, the angels, and the animals (Mk 1:13),
Jesus turned to preaching God's kingdom in word and deed, beginning not back in 'his own country' at Nazareth, but at the
Lake. In modern parlance, we may say that Jesus 'moved again'.
He had moved from Nazareth to the wilderness, now he trav-
elled to his new home, at Capernaum on the Lake. Salvation
ecology gleams in Matthew's melodious description of green
and golden Galilee, to which Jesus moved: 'Leaving Nazareth he
went and dwelt in Capernaum by the sea, in the territory of
Zebulun and Naphtali, that what was spoken by the prophet
Isaiah might be fulfilled; "The land of Zebulun and the land of
Naphtali, toward the sea, across the Jordan, Galilee of the
Gentiles".' (Mt 4:13-15). I have wandered through the haunting

ruins of Capernaum, by that sea, now a much visited ghost
town, a place of pilgrims, which until this century was little
more than Tell Hum, intermittently visited by Bedouin and their
grazing stock. One October morning, when there were no other
visitors, I sat among the ruins of the houses near the lake, a few
metres from shore, watching the wild birds, each known and
given its food in due season, flitting around the stones and
scrub. Suddenly from the south-west, the first winter rains
swept gently across the sea and Capernaum. This was that welcome early rain Jesus knew, which he included in his parables,
and which he redeemed, with ourselves and with all the rains
and waters of the earth. That October morning, when I thought I
was alone and unseen, concluded with some humorous relief.
As I stood up and walked from Capernaum, a young, bearded
Orthodox monk said, 'You Anglos are very strange. You sit in
the rain.'

There was – and is – more than shore, basalt ruins, and winter rains to Capernaum. Like Nazareth, Capernaum is a protected,
fertile, sun blessed site. It enjoys a small harbour with sea life, on
the north-west corner of the lake, which is about 32 miles in cir-
cumference. In its hinterland, Capernaum rivals Nazareth's sur-
rounding plain: cereals, vines, olives, and top fruit flourish.
Chorazin, visible in the hilly north, is mentioned in the Talmud
for its excellent grain, which still grows wild around the ruins.
The hallowed Mount, which Jesus certainly knew, and probably
visited often, where Matthew seems to place his famous sermon,
abounds with plantations. The blue lake, like many similar
Michigan lakes, yet unique in all the earth, the representative
lake, is a teeming ecosystem, blessed with fish and birds, raptors
and scavengers, reeds and tamarisks, a different but no less lush
biodiversity than that of lower Galilee. In Jesus' time the protected
harbour sheltered small boats, and was an inland port, in so far
as so small a lake could be said to have a port. Capernaum was
near Herod Philip's Gaulanitis, and was therefore a base for tax
gatherers and soldiers. We have no written evidence that Jesus
visited the large Hellenic settlements, such as Sepphoris four

miles north of Nazareth, and Tiberias, Herod's gleaming capital
on the lake. John Meier comments, 'As far as we know, within
Galilee his ministry (as well as verbal references) was restricted
to traditional Jewish villages and towns: Nazareth, Capernaum,
Cana, Nain, and Chorazin. Within Galilee proper, the Hellenistic
cities of Sepphoris and Tiberias are notable by their absence on
Jesus' itinerary.'[2]

On Earth as in Heaven
When he lived in Capernaum, Jesus often retired to quiet places,
in the hinterland or elsewhere in Galilee, either alone or with a
few close disciples, perhaps fishermen. Of his closest disciples,
C. H. Dodd wrote, 'His most intimate associates, or at any rate
those about whom we are told the most, were partners in a fish-
ery business, owning their own boats and employing labour.'[3]
His ministry was itinerant, especially to Galilean villages, where
he preached the forthcoming kingdom and taught, healed, and,
where a synagogue was available, read in the synagogue. His
healings and exorcisms were of whole persons, body and spirit,
and included the natural world in which people are embedded.
His compassion touched soldiers, outcasts, foreigners, and
women, and attracted attention. His lifestyle, or *praxis*, was a
central ingredient of his preaching. Jesus' way of living, described by Matthew, was one of deep trust in his heavenly
Father's providence. He preached, not 'economic growth' nor
'progress', but reliance on God, restraint, sufficiency, sustainability. In words now famous, he said:

> Look at the birds of the air; they neither sow nor reap nor
> gather into barns, and yet your heavenly Father feeds them.
> Are you not of more value than they? And which of you by
> being anxious can add one cubit to his span of life? And why
> are you anxious about clothing? Consider the lilies of the
> field, how they grow; they neither toil nor spin; yet I tell you,
> even Solomon in all his glory was not arrayed like one of
> these (Mt 6:26-29).

People, God's representatives on earth, as God's image, are especially important and responsible within an earth community in which all creatures, every flower and sparrow, are known and provided for.

The main point of Jesus' preaching was the coming of God's kingdom, on earth as in heaven. A contemporary Jewish prayer, used in synagogues, reflects imminent expectations then current in Palestine: 'May he establish his kingdom in your lifetime and in your days and in the lifetime of all the house of Israel, even speedily and at a near time.'[4] For ourselves, in globalised, consumerist democracies, even where there are ceremonial heads of state, it is difficult to envision a monarchical kingdom. In Jesus' time, the ideals of good kingship included responsibilities for the flourishing rain and fertility. The wild animals kneel before him (Ps 72:3, 6, 9, 16). John Eaton writes, 'This king, exalted because of his pity for the humble, is depicted in Adam-like messianic harmony with the animals (rather as in the great prophecy, Is 11:1-9).'[5] In contemporary Jewish expectations, therefore, the kingdom is not a soul heaven 'above', but includes the earth. New Testament scholar Graham Stanton observes, 'The kingdom of God is God's kingly rule, the time and place where God's power and will hold sway.'[6] Jesus preached God's kingdom using metaphors and parables drawn from food growing, as in his fields at Nazareth and in the Capernaum hinterland. The Jesus of the gospels was sensitive to the changing seasons, weather, seeds, soil, growth, harvest, and the treasure of local rural wisdom about working with a local biosystem. God's rain, he noted, falls on just and unjust. We may ponder, with reverence, two questions: 1) do Jesus' nature metaphors also teach the inherent value of the natural world itself? and 2) to what extent is the whole soil community, including our responsible co-operation with it, within God's already arriving kingdom? V. G. John, of Bishop's College, Kolkata, India, says Jesus' choice of images from nature teaches nature's own value:

> Jesus' choosing to use the images derived from nature in his communication of the divine rule indicts the human attempts to measure the worth of nature in terms of its utility

value ... As a means of communicating divine activity,
Nature has its own value. It does not merely exist for the sake
of humanity, but for its own sake and as witness to God and
his benevolent activity of care.[7]

As God's representative, within his kingdom, people are like the
ideal shepherd king of the Jewish scriptures. Like a priest taken
from among people, to serve people, the king is not a foreigner
nor an outsider from a different community, but one taken from
his own brethren, who holds his lambs in his arms: 'One from
among your brethren you shall set as king over you; you may
not put a foreigner over you, who is not your brother' (Deut
17:15). Ignatius Loyola, in a synthesis of Jesus' preaching, illuminated by his insights at the Cardoner river near Manresa, describes discipleship as poverty and labour, in imitation of Christ
the King. In feudal language, Ignatius presents, to our imagination, Christ the King addressing us now: 'Whoever desires to
come with me must be contented with the food that I eat, with
the drink and the clothing that I have, etc. In like manner he
must labour as I do during the day, and watch during the night,
etc., in order that afterwards he may have part with me in the
victory, as he has had in the hard work.'[8] As God's image, servant shepherd kings, we live, and serve Christ and his created
community, as he lived and served on earth.

Light on the Lake

Jesus' teaching, including his praxis, his healing miracles, and
shared meals, intimated to some contemporaries the arrival of
God's kingdom. Puzzled at reports reaching him, the Baptist
sent emissaries to inquire if Jesus was indeed the awaited One.
Jesus replied symbolically, sending word that the blind see, the
lame walk, the deaf hear, the poor hear the good news (Mt 11:2-
6). In Jewish expectations, to which Jesus referred, these miracles are connected with abundant water, and the flowering of
the desert. 'Waters shall break forth in the wilderness, and
streams in the desert; the burning sand shall become a pool, and
the thirsty ground springs of water' (Is 35:6-7; cf. Is 36:16-17). A

curious contemporary exception were the Essenes of the Dead
Sea, who both excluded handicapped people from that community and, of necessity, used not living water but cisterns.

Communal meals, integral to Jesus' teaching, symbolised,
and inaugurated, the kingdom of God on earth. I think these frequent shared meals have enormous, still unrecognised, significance in Jesus' message, and *in our continuation* of his preaching,
and in our practice today. For, as we have noticed, preaching includes practice – and practice reinforces preaching. Jesus' meals
made many points. His words at and about them reinforced the
meaning of the meals. At the eucharist, the memorial itself
preaches and remembers Jesus, all that he is, all that he believed,
all that he taught; and the homily reinforces this liturgical remembrance. In the words of the Lima Report, an ecumenical
agreed statement, 'Since the anamnesis (i.e. remembrance) of
Christ is the very content of the preached Word as it is of the eucharistic meal, each reinforces the other. The celebration of the
eucharist properly includes the proclamation of the Word.'
From Jesus' shared meals, no less than from his life in Nazareth
fields, and the parables, we learn how to co-operate with God
and the soil, and how to care for the whole soil community
which provides bread, 'which earth has given and human hands
have made', and all the cereals, vegetables, fruit, bees and vines,
fish and animals of the kingdom which nourish us now, and remain with us transfigured in our future. Noel Dermot
O'Donoghue writes, reverently and also provocatively, 'Indeed,
every Christian knows that the last supper of Jesus was a sym-
posium or drinking party in which the valediction was the passing around of a wine glass with the words: "Take and drink …
and do this always in remembrance of me".'[9] Significantly, Jesus
dined with people unwelcome to many Jews, including tax gatherers and women of the night, 'Truly, I say to you, the tax collectors and the harlots go into the kingdom of God before you' (Mt
21:31).

One meal in particular, an outdoor feeding of a large crowd,
left a deep impression on the first disciples, who recounted it

orally, in slightly different versions, and included it in all four
gospels, in duplicate in two of them. All accounts agree there
was a multiplication of loaves and fishes, although details vary,
possibly for symbolic reasons. We just noticed the connotations
of the flowering of the wilderness and abundant water in Jesus'
healing. The wilderness meal also may connote that flowering
and abundance. Although we do not know precisely what happened that memorable day in the wilderness, nor the actual
numbers of people, loaves, fishes, or baskets of remnants, we do
know that such meals were common events for Jesus and his followers in quiet rural places. We also know from our own experience, that food can and does almost 'just happen' or, through
someone's generosity, appears almost surprisingly at our own
communal meals, picnics, and celebrations. Fertile fields and
fish from the lake, were at hand to Jesus and his disciples, at and
near the lake. The feeding, like the healing ministry and the
parables, foreshadows the flowering of creatures in God's kingdom. The Capernaum fertility, the grapes and grain of the hill-
sides, fish dried and salted for transport to Jerusalem and
Sepphoris, or retained for local use – all this abundance contributed to Jesus' meals. The feeding of four or five thousand – in
any scenario a large number of followers, and hearers – with fish
and bread left over after the meal, is ecologically evocative. The
kingdom of God in Jesus risen is like the flowering of the desert,
a golden harvest, a cosmic liturgy where, in Gerard Manley
Hopkins' words:

Heavenly vales so thick shall stand

With corn that they shall laugh and sing.

These meals of Jesus have pointers for our practice. We symbolise, anticipate, and in a sense inaugurate the kingdom in our fellowship meals, and in our organic gardens, or beds, where we
prepare for meals. Should we not share meals more? With fellow
Christians, and with others, including some who sometimes
may feel excluded? And should we not offer hospitality more, in
our homes, to neighbours, friends, and fellow worshippers?

Nature Miracles and Other Faiths

The gospels include nature miracles – perhaps the feeding of the multitude is one – which are partly legendary, proclaiming Jesus as Lord and Saviour. Even wind and sea obey him! The nature miracles, legendary or not, disclose Jesus as more than an ordinary prophet and teacher, more even than healer and exorcist – although he was all these. There is one nature miracle I want to recall here. We are all familiar with the calming of the storm, from childhood Sunday Schools, catechetics, gospel readings, or religious studies. There is something particularly gripping, even dramatic, about Jesus resting on a cushion in a small boat and, when asked, majestically calming a frightening storm with a brief, if firm, command. Mastery of the water, as we noticed in theological art, is a divine prerogative. Yet Jesus also comes through here as appealingly human – resting on a cushion with close friends in a small boat on the lake. A similar first-century boat, recovered recently near Magdala, is on display at Gennesaret today. The calming story connotes the expulsion of evil, the healing of nature, and includes water – in a word, salvation ecology and salvation history. I noted that the nature miracles are often partly legendary, a narrative commentary on the Old Testament perhaps, not historical in our post-Enlightenment sense of history. The calming story may be a coded commentary on some verses in Psalm 107:

For he commanded, and raised the stormy wind,
which lifted up the waves of the sea.
They mounted up to heaven, they went down to the depths;
their courage melted away in their evil plight;
they reeled and staggered like drunken men,
and were at their wits' end.
Then they cried to the lord in their trouble,
and he delivered them from their distress;
he made the storm be still,
and the waves of the sea were hushed (Ps 107:25-29).

Our Lord's hushing of the waves contrasts with the hapless Jonah who was also caught in a storm. Only when the sailors threw Jonah overboard did the waves calm. Jonah then went to Nineveh, where he resented God's mercy towards the Ninevites. God corrected Jonah, saying he should pity the Ninevites, who knew not their left hand from their right, and also their many cattle (Jon 4:11).

Jesus' preaching, and his cures, were directed primarily to 'the lost sheep of the house of Israel'. But, as his Jonah references show, he did not exclude people of other races and religions. The kingdom included many from other races, colours, and cultures: 'Many will come from east and west and sit at table with Abraham, Isaac, and Jacob in the kingdom of heaven' (Mt 8:11). Jesus left clues about inter-religious inclusion, as he did about the inclusion of the whole soil community in the kingdom, for us to ponder in our time of globalisation, environmental crises, and inter-religious convergence. There is pity in the Jewish scriptures for people other than the Hebrew tribes, and for their animals. Jesus referred several times to the Jonah story, perhaps hinting at the inclusion of other peoples in salvation. He said that as Jonah became a sign to the Ninevites, 'so will the Son of Man be to this generation' (Lk 11:30). Although Jesus went primarily to the Jewish people, there are scattered hints of universalism in his words and deeds, of inclusion of peoples 'from east and west'. Within our Christian story are the Good Samaritan, Naaman the Syrian, the Zarephath widow, Jairus and his daughter, the Samaritan woman at the well and the Syro-Phoenician woman, her daughter, and the dogs beneath the table. Finally, will come the good thief, and the believing centurion from the city where Caesar ruled. The Jordan experience, the communal meals, the nature miracles, and the parables include the whole earth community.

The Shrine of Pan

Jesus' brief ministry on earth climaxed in the southern foothills of Mount Hermon, in territory associated with the tribe of Dan. I never realised until I went there just how ecologically evocative 'the district of Caesarea Philippi' is. The spring day we were there, Barbara and I even met some new age pilgrims, reminiscent of Stonehenge druids in June, gathered around the visible source of that life-giving river. A subterranean aquifer springs from the foothills, gathering and begetting that awesome river that widens and rushes downstream into the rift valley. The hills themselves abound with flora, including herbs, olives, walnuts, and oak. I still treasure, on my bedside table, the husk of a Caesarea Philippi acorn, which I found beneath an oak. Oaks, with their leafy banners, embellished with acorn pendants, and their amazingly diverse wildlife residents are, at least in some biosystems, the prince of trees. (Date palms might claim that honour in the Sinai.) The mountain invites reverence for nature. Hence the visiting druids! Herod Philip called the settlement Caesarea Philippi, attempting to rival his father's maritime Caesarea. In the Byzantine period, there was a basilica where there had been a pagan shrine and temples. The Byzantines called the district Caesarea Panias. Traces of the shrine, and of the name, remain in the present Banias. Somewhere in that verdant district, Jesus instructed his disciples about himself, and his mission, as he then understood it.

In the happily vanished polemical era from the Council of Trent (1545-1563) to Vatican II, a favourite 'proof text' of Catholics was Matthew 16:18, attributed to Jesus at Caesarea Philippi: 'You are Peter, and on this rock I will build my church, and the powers of death shall not prevail against it' (Mt 16:18). During preparations for the latter council, the Canadian bishops had as their *peritus*, or theologian, biblical scholar David Stanley SJ, who was renowned at the time for his work on Jesus' death and resurrection. David Stanley visited the Jesuit theologate in Indiana, where I was studying at the time. Whenever a distinguished visitor shared our roof and table, we always asked her, or him, to address us student 'theologians', which they usually did. I still remember David Stanley's talk, a brilliant exposition of the titles of Jesus. He explained how, in contemporary Jewish culture, 'Son of Man' could be a more transcendent title than 'Son of God', a debate which persists among biblical scholars to this day.[10] During questions an always thoughtful former GI, veteran of some battles after Normandy, tabled a question that did not directly address David Stanley's lecture. 'What about Matthew 16:18?' he asked. Stanley graciously shifted gear, answering the question in some detail. We were all interested in Stanley's learned answer. For Matthew 16:18 was not only a favourite text, it recurred in several parts of the course in ecclesiology which I was studying that year. The text sometimes surfaced in examinations, not only at the year's end, but in the comprehensive, or *ad gradum*, oral examination, in Latin, after seven years of philosophy and theology. The passage comes after Peter's confession of faith, in Jesus' commission to Peter, which Matthew places near the ancient shrine of Pan. Matthew even places the name change, from Simon to Cephas, or Peter, at that time and place. 'And I tell you, you are Peter, and on this rock I will build my church, and the powers of death shall not prevail against it' (Mt 16:18). The verse, in universal Latin, adorns the chancel wall in the Catholic church of St Peter, in Tiberias, a building imaginatively, if rather triumphantly, shaped like a barque or boat of Peter. One pastor, an Australian Franciscan, told me with understandable pride, that his was Jesus' own parish. He said so many Palestinian Christians had been 'ethnically cleansed' in 1948 that his parish extended far north, beyond Jesus' Capernaum into Lebanon. It was a joy, especially on Sundays, to worship with remnant Palestinian Christians who had travelled some distance to Mass. During Peter's lifetime and in the first Christian communities, Peter's primacy probably developed slowly, and certainly not legalistically, as the first Christians gradually ordered their ministry after the resurrection. The identification of the present Petrine office, or servant papacy, with Peter and with Caesarea Philippi, has foundation in Matthew's gospel. Fortunately, the papacy is again gradually becoming what it was, and should be, a primacy of love, honour, service, and humility, which unites, rather than divides, Christians.

The relationship of the Petrine primacy with the source of the

Jordan, at Banias, has potential, now beginning to be tapped, for ecumenical and inter-religious ecology. Notice again those new age pilgrims at the spring, most of whom seemed to be Jews. Nearing the end of his own Petrine ministry, Pope John Paul II called for an 'ecological conversion', and signed a joint declaration with the ecumenical Patriarch about Christian responsibility for the earth. Whether in Dolomite villages, as a young Pope on walking holidays, or as an elderly Pope at home, the Polish Pope preached often about Christian love and care for the earth, once describing Psalm 148 as 'a cosmic alleluia involving everything and everyone in divine praise'. Perhaps by coincidence the 1994 *Catechism of the Catholic Church* includes a letter of commendation from the Pope, and a logo from a tombstone in the catacomb of Domitilla. The logo portrays a good shepherd, with lamb and staff, playing panpipes beneath the Tree of Life. Here we have an intriguing stimulus for our imaginations – and our hopes: the ancient shrine of Pan, and the successors of Peter, the Ecumenical Patriarch, Archbishop of Canterbury, and Free Church leaders as servants of the whole soil community.

Transfiguration

The last journey south, from Caesarea Philippi through Galilee to Jerusalem, seems to have been sombre. The natural world, as in April today, was beautiful, fragrant, in full spring, like the river itself, yellow with wild flowers, and golden with barley ready for spring harvest, with birds and animals migrating, and mating, nesting, and giving birth to new life. Jesus and his followers knew that Jerusalem would be less verdant, less welcoming than the soil community of Mount Hermon. Somewhere on the journey, an experience or epiphany of Jesus in glory happened. The synoptics say the setting was a mountain top, for mountains are the symbolic setting for epiphanies, intuitions and intimations of God's glory. The Father's voice, we are told, came again from a cloud, the symbolic abode of God's hidden presence among us. The Father's words are reminiscent of the Jordan epiphany, 'This is my beloved Son; listen to him' (Mk

9:7). Moses and Elijah also appear briefly, respectively representing salvation history and ecology. Unexpectedly, Jesus appears transcendent, God's glory shines through Jesus' body and clothes, he 'was transfigured before them, and his garments became glistening intensely white, as no fuller on earth could bleach them' (Mk 9:2-3). Peter, wishing to prolong the experience, suggests they erect booths as at grape harvest, in one of many naïve lapses by leaders in the Jesus movement. For a shining moment only, at the mountain, Jesus appears for what he is, the reconciling Presence of God among us. It is impossible to reconstruct what historically happened that day, which the gospels describe as a metamorphosis, or transfiguration, when, briefly on that mountain God's glory shone through Jesus, revealing who he was. The scene is a model, and symbol, or paradigm, for each of us in our own life mission, how we should take responsibility for matter, the whole earth community. Like the Virgin Mary, the iconographers, the saints, artists, poets, musicians, and Christian environmentalists, each of us 'this one work has to do – let all God's glory through'. Our ministry, our mission in life, is to let be, to let God transform and transfigure the earth, through our lives, our bodies, our words and actions, conducting a 'cosmic alleluia' with all our fellow creatures. Our responsibility, or dominion, is to represent God on earth, to be the explicit voice of earth's praise of God, 'liturgising the cosmos', to love, honour, even serve, our fellow creatures, who glorify God with us. With the Laon oxen, and their craftsmen, we are all, symbolically, hilltoppers, letting God's glory shine through our lives, on our particular mountain, letting every hill be a 'crowned hill', a place refulgent with God's glory. We let God's glory through when we honour matter, as well as invisible creatures. In St John Damascene's famous words, 'I shall not cease to honour matter, for through matter my salvation was accomplished.'

The Transition to the Temple
For every Jew the Temple was special, the place of God's pres-

ence, where heaven and earth meet. As he approached the city, on that last journey, Jesus headed purposefully for that numinous centre of Judaism. He approached the Temple through the Mount of Olives which, then as now, in April would have been fragrant with herbs and wild flowers, musical with wind hymning through olive trees, bees working and birds singing in the branches. From Bethany, Jesus sent disciples to bring a donkey, perhaps borrowed from the beloved disciple. When he entered the city, sitting on that gentle animal upon which none had ridden, people spread cloaks and branches in his path. Many of the Jews, including the aristocracy, would have recalled the words of the prophet Zechariah, 'Lo, your king comes to you; triumphant and victorious is he, humble and riding on an ass, on a colt the foal of an ass' (Zech 9:9). Hosannas rang around the ears of Jesus and of the animal. When Jewish leaders objected to the acclamation, Jesus quoted Psalm 8: 'Out of the mouth of babes and sucklings thou hast brought perfect praise' (Ps 8:2; Mt 21:16). This psalm summarises the Genesis creation story, portraying people as God's representatives, with responsibilities for the earth community, which is not to be worshipped, nor is it a human possession. People are shepherd kings, who glorify God, while holding God's lambs in their arms (Ps 8:1 & 9).

When he entered the Temple, Jesus acted symbolically, and provocatively. What the displacement of tables and rebuke of merchants symbolised was that the new, awaited presence of God was here, in Jesus himself. Jesus was – and is – the living water which flows from the Temple precincts, nourishing the Tree of Life, whose leaves feed, and heal, the nations (Ezek 47:12). The Jewish establishment, mainly an entrenched group of priests, were annoyed and felt threatened by this kingdom committed layman who aroused expectations. He had challenged them. They would respond in due course, which would be soon. Jesus departed through the olive mountain, for a final meal with close disciples at Bethany. The following day he would return for a communal meal, in Jerusalem, the last supper of them all, which we commemorate in our eucharists, awaiting his return, letting God's glory through.

Notes:

1. *The Autobiography of St Ignatius Loyola,* Joseph F. O'Callaghan, trans., John C. Olin, ed. (New York: Fordham University Press, 1992), p. 39.
2. Meier, *A Marginal Jew,* Vol. I, p. 284.
3. Dodd, *The Founder of Christianity,* p. 127.
4. Graham Stanton, *The Gospels and Jesus* (Oxford: Oxford University Press, 1989), p. 194.
5. John Eaton, 'Bible and Animals, Prejudice in Translation', *The Ark* (Winter 2003), pp. 12-13; cf. Edward P. Echlin, 'Meat Eating and Vegetarianism in the Ark', Ibid., pp. 7-9.
6. *The Gospels and Jesus,* p. 196.
7. V. J. John, 'Kingdom of God and Ecology: A Parabolic Perspective', *Bangalore Theological Forum,* Vol. XXXIV, 1 (June 2002), p. 113.
8. Ignatius Loyola, *Spiritual Exercises,* p. 33.
9. Noel Dermot O'Donoghue, *The Angels Keep their Ancient Places, Reflections on Celtic Spirituality* (Edinburgh: T. & T. Clark, 2001), p. 41.
10. Graham Stanton, *Gospel Truth? New Light on Jesus and the Gospels* (London: Harper Collins, 1995), pp. 151-155.

CHAPTER SIX

Cosmic Cross, Cosmic Circle

He stretched out his hands on the cross,
that he might embrace the ends of the world;
for this Golgotha is the very centre of the earth ...
He stretched forth human hands,
who by his spiritual hands had established the heaven.
(Cyril of Jerusalem, *Catechetical Lecture* 13)

Holy Week, commemorating the last week of Jesus in Jerusalem, crowned by Easter, was a climactic week when I grew up in a predominantly Jewish and Christian neighbourhood in northwest Detroit. Easter, the 'eighth day' of new creation, was preceded by a six-week anticipatory Lent, in which we made small sacrifices, 'giving something up', in solidarity with Jesus who suffered in his humanity on the cross. On Ash Wednesday, and on Fridays, we abstained from meat but ate fish, eggs, and dairy products. Wednesdays, and especially Fridays, in Lent were busy times for the many 'seafood' restaurants clustered around the southern Great Lakes. Sundays and St Patrick's Day (17th March) interrupted the routine, when we enjoyed some chocolate, or ice cream and, at least in Irish American households, a 'boiled dinner' of kosher corned beef, cabbage, carrots and potatoes. Holy Week began on Palm Sunday, with the blessing and distribution of new palms, a short procession, and a long gospel, usually Mark's passion account, at Mass, during which we stood, in compassion with Jesus' suffering. The climactic triduum (the last three days of Holy Week), at least in Gesu church, began in anticipation on Wednesday evening with Tenebrae. At the ancient service of Tenebrae, clergy and religious and lay ministers chant Matins and Lauds, on Wednesday to Friday evenings in Holy Week. Tenebraes, with their one-by-one extinguished candles – one extinguished after each psalm – were

chanted in the large sanctuary of Gesu church, which architects
designed with Tenebrae in mind. Religious priests and brothers,
from the parish, from the University of Detroit, and from the
nearby Jesuit Preparatory School, gathered at Gesu for Tenebrae.
The church became darker, as the candles gradually were extinguished. The service ended literally with a loud clap, as the
chanters closed their books in unison, and silently departed.
Only years later did I realise that the extinguished candles, the
darkness, and the book clap signified cosmic involvement, even
cosmic compassion, at Golgotha, where our redemption was accomplished in suffering (Mt 27:51).

There were many Holy Week services in parish churches and
chapels, and in the religious houses, convents, schools, and hos-
pitals, spread around our neighbourhood. That meant altar boys
were in temporary demand, and spread thin. In my last three
years at junior school, I served two years at St Mary Reparatrix,
a cloistered convent, where sisters lived silently, sang Divine
Office, and hosted retreats for women. My final year I served at
Marygrove, a girls' college a bicycle ride away, staffed by a community of teaching sisters. On Good Friday, from twelve to
three, most of us remained quietly at home, until we were old
enough to join our parents at Tre Ore.

Years later, in Jesuit houses of study we celebrated Holy
Week services in our own 'domestic' chapel. Even with exams
approaching, ordinary routine (*de more*) was suspended in that
early spring week, when we spent long hours in chapel. Later
still, I preached at Tre Ore, at St Peter's and Paul's Church in
downtown Detroit, the city's oldest church, with reminders in
its fabric of Detroit's French and Indian past. I still remember
feeling daunted, as a young and inexperienced preacher, when
my own provincial and some familiar councillors, judges, and
other civil servants and professionals filed in quietly. They too
suspended ordinary activities, and the courts closed, during
those three hours when God was on the cross.

The earth – and cosmic – dimension of our redemption was
included, but not emphasised, in Holy Week. Paul Evdokimov,

an Orthodox liturgist, writes, 'The church's calendar and the cycle of offerings sanctify and fill with meaning the elements of time and the march of history.'[1] Tre Ore, and the other services of that exceptional week and triduum express compassion, contrition, and gratitude for what God has done for his creatures, especially in those last hours in Jerusalem, reconciling to himself all things, on earth as in heaven. While we did not emphasise cosmic redemption, 'all things visible and invisible' were there, in the water, palms, bread and wine, the donkey of Palm Sunday, in the candles, darkness, and clap of Tenebrae, culminating in the ecologically rich *Exultet*, and oil, water, candles, fire, and flowers, of Holy Saturday and Easter. As Yves Congar OP, used to say, our whole faith is in the liturgy.

People ask – and we all wonder – why earth inclusion is not emphasised more? Where did we go wrong? Matthew's gospel vividly includes darkness, and cosmic quakes, as 'all creation wept', when Jesus died on the cross. John says that Jesus was crucified and buried in a garden. All early testimony includes continuity, and new creation, in Jesus' death and triumph. His blood flows onto the first Adam beneath the cross. But these hints were only sporadically appreciated in the Christian centuries. Some early writers, influenced by Aristotle, say that other earth beings exist principally, or even exclusively, for people, because we alone reason, we are God's image. In the early Christian centuries, however, other creatures were recognised as creatures, even if their presence glorifying God with us was neglected. Renaissance men emphasised human freedom but not the dignity of other creatures. Nor did the era of discovery correlate our own deep cosmic roots with the ecological dimensions of other religions. Since the seventeenth-century scientific awakening, scientists have thought themselves destined to 'bend', 'master', and 'conquer' nature, even to modify plants and animals for human convenience, and 'progress'.

A remarkable condensation of the last millennium's credulity towards the progress myth, despite the increasingly obvious unsustainable damage to the earth, is encapsulated in one sentence in Harry S. Truman's 1949 inaugural address: 'We must embark on a new type of program for making the benefits of our scientific advances, with industrial progress, available for the improvement and growth of underdeveloped areas.' In brief, industrialised, consumerist, capitalist democracies must bring western mode 'progress' and 'sustainable development' to other cultures, including those who genuinely live in sustainable sufficiency. Also in 1949, the literary critic Cyril Connolly said, 'It is closing time in the gardens of the west. From now on, an artist will be judged only by the resonance of his solitude or the quality of his despair.' The despair was reflected in obsessive individualism, consumerism, family disintegration, and a rush of psychologised spiritualities that still abound in numerous summer schools, 'spirituality centres', 'inner sabbaticals', and 'institutes of human sexuality'.

Fortunately, in this new millennium there are bright harbingers of disengagement from the progress myth, from individualism, and from psychologised spiritualities. Inspired in part by the resourcement, returning to the sources, of recent French theology, many in the church are rediscovering the holism of the Bible, the liturgy, and the early church, and are including the earth in theology, spiritualities, liturgies, and structures, and in art, and parish life. The gardens of the west are again opening – and their fare often is organic. It may be no coincidence that Lent, especially St Patrick's Day and Holy Week, is the season for sowing new potatoes, a harbinger, with newly sown shallots and broad beans, of another spring and, after spring, of harvest, symbolic of new creation. In the following few pages, I will notice some of the earth inclusion in Jesus' last days – and our response.

The Last Meals
The Bethany meal, with close friends and disciples, was the penultimate of Jesus' many communal meals, which symbolised and inaugurated the kingdom. The meal at Bethany is especially remembered as the meal when Mary of Bethany anointed Jesus

with precious ointment. The fragrant spikenard, or myrrh, integrates flora of distant bioregions in Jesus' reconciliation of the cosmos. The anointing was poignant, because both Jesus and Mary realised it could be for his burial, especially after the unconventional entrance on the donkey, the salutations of the crowds, and the disruption at the Temple. It was doubly poignant when Judas missed the burial and ecological connotations, and departed angrily into the night (Mk 14:4-5; 10:11).

In the morning Jesus sent disciples to arrange another meal, this time in Jerusalem, during the celebrations of Passover and Unleavened Bread. We cannot be sure who hosted the Last Supper, although recently the beloved disciple has been suggested.[2] Many earth creatures, including a lamb, herbs, fruit, and vegetables, were included in the meal. Bread and wine represent the whole soil community at the Last Supper, as they do in our eucharists. Jesus broke and shared 'bread which earth has given, and human hands have made', and 'wine, fruit of the vine and work of human hands'. That final meal must be set within the context of the many shared meals, hosted by Jesus, which would continue after his resurrection, and which we continue until he returns (cf. Mk 2:15; Lk 24:13-35). The Last Supper, though not without foreboding, was hopeful; it symbolised continuity with the future kingdom – for Jesus said he would drink wine again, in God's kingdom, and that we should celebrate memorials of him, which we do in our eucharists (Lk 22:19-20; 1 Cor 11:23-26).

The Olive Garden

After that last shared meal, Jesus and his closest disciples walked across the Kidron wadi, to a favourite 'lonely place', near the foot of the Mount. John says, 'Jesus went there often with his disciples' (Jn 18:2; Lk 23:39; 21:37). During the short descent, Jesus predicted that his disciples would soon forsake him. When Peter expostulated, Jesus gave his famous rejoinder, 'Before the cock crows twice, you will deny me three times' (Mk 14:30). That prophecy, as we have known since childhood, was soon fulfilled. Sometimes passed over, in our embarrassment with Judas and now Peter, and seeing ourselves in Peter, is the association of that beautiful fowl with the last hours of our Saviour. A vigilant fowl, alone among God's earth creatures, cried out at the betrayal of God. It may be a coincidence, but is worth noticing, that in Roman times the rooster, like bread and wine, symbolised fertility, as in a funerary frieze discovered near Lyons, from Roman Gaul, of a lad with cat and rooster. The sheep of the Mount also enjoy inclusion in the passion. Jesus even quotes Zachariah, 'I will strike the shepherd, and the sheep will be scattered' (Mt 14:27; Zech 13:7). When visiting Gethsemane, I noticed sheep browsing serenely on the lower flanks of the Mount, some, remarkably, with small birds on their backs. Despite the stench and roar of cars below and jets above, the gnarled trees are quietly serene, resonant with floral diversity, insect and bird life and song. I did not see the shepherd, but could sense his presence somewhere in the shade of the olives. There is at Gethsemane, especially in spring, an almost tangible intimation of Presence, as there is also at the Lake. Certain persons, primarily the incarnate Person who is our God and Saviour, long after they have departed physically, live in our corporate memories, or better approach us anew, from the future mists in certain places and at certain times. Francis Thompson seems to touch delicately upon these indescribable intimations that all of us experience:

Yet ever and anon a trumpet sounds
From the hid battlements of Eternity;
Those shaken mists a space unsettle, then
Round the half-glimps'd turrets slowly wash again.
(*The Hound of Heaven*)

A Jesuit scholastic and English teacher, now within those 'hid battlements', and buried at Colombiere College, Clarkston, Michigan, introduced me to *The Hound of Heaven* when I was in high school, and also to a comparatively obscure little ballad on Gethsemane, by Sidney Lanier. I kept the ballad, and later, when myself a Jesuit scholastic, typed it out. I still have the typed

copy, in my study, on very yellow paper. The ballad captures
something of the Presence, the pathos, and the salvation ecology
of Gethsemane:

> Into the woods my Master went,
> Clean forspent, forspent.
> Into the woods my Master came,
> Forspent with love and shame.
>
> But the olives were not blind to Him,
> The little grey leaves were kind to Him,
> The thorn tree had a mind to Him
> When into the woods He came
>
> Out of the woods my Master went,
> And He was well content.
> Out of the woods my Master came,
> Content with death and shame.
>
> When death and shame would woo Him last
> From under the trees they drew Him last;
> Twas on a tree they slew Him – last
> When out of the woods He came.
> *(Ballad of Trees and the Master)*

The Galilee olives are in a sunny, rather westerly position, as the
Roman agriculturist, Cato, said olives should be.[3] Pilgrims, including myself, would like to think the ancient, gnarled, silvery
green trees of that numinous place are the same trees that wel-
comed and sheltered Jesus that April (or Nisan) night, and
whose roots drink his blood and perspiration. But, despite their
gnarled antiquity, they are not. The Romans felled most
Jerusalem trees in AD 70. Nevertheless, by the fourth century
Gethsemane was replanted and regenerated, again an olive garden, and now a place of pilgrimage. Bishop Cyril of Jerusalem
remarked in that century, 'Gethsemane bears witness, the place
where the betrayal occurred.' Tree felling can be vindictive and
unwise. Felling healthy trees, especially fruit trees, should be
done rarely, and only with proportionate reason. Whether in
today's illegally occupied West Bank, or in an overpopulated

island, we do well to heed the biblically grounded wisdom of
Jonathan Gorsky:

> Traditional Jewish law teaches us that we do not destroy
> houses and we do not uproot citrus groves and olive trees. If
> a house is built illegally the owner might be penalised, but
> we do not demolish the building. If, and only if, trees are
> being used as cover for active hostilities then, after due and
> proper consideration, action might be taken, but if it dam-
> ages innocent people then they must be taken care of, and
> those who would destroy trees are asked to recall that, when
> a fruit tree is destroyed, a cry can be heard from one end of
> the world to the other.[4]

John's gospel notes that Jesus and his disciples crossed 'the
Kidron Valley where there is a garden' (Jn 18:11). John may be
hinting at parallels – or coincidences – between Jesus and King
David, who also crossed 'the winter flowing Kidron'. David
wept on the Mount, because of the perfidy of Ahithophel, a
trusted companion who betrayed him. Like Judas, Ahithophel
went on to hang himself; the two are the only biblical persons so
to die (2 Sam 17:23). Jesus' own internal sufferings we call 'the
agony in the garden'. In the garden, says Luke, he perspired
drops like blood. As we noted, few places on earth are more suffused with Jesus' presence than that small community of olive
trees and their companion ecosystem. In one sense of continued
Presence, at least, Jesus is preserved there, in his tears, perspiration, and blood, where he remains, in his fullness, within the
hillside, beneath the trees, now and forever. Mark adds that,
when the soldiers arrived, a young man, dressed only in a loincloth, slipped the arresters and fled naked, his loincloth in their
hands. Scholars speculate endlessly on that brief scene. I suggest
that the young fugitive symbolises Mark himself – and all of us –
who, in our different ways, desert Jesus. The young man would
have suffered his own torments that Passover. As do we, when
we flee Jesus, and creation's restraints, for globalised consumerism. The shoppers' mall is a lonely temple.

The Other Trials

The last hour in the usually peaceful olive garden, far from being a respite, was itself a 'trial', experienced by Jesus as a hard cup, and a hard hour. After his arrest, Jesus endured still more, also painful, trials. Whether before the Jewish elite, the Roman governor, or Herod the King, Jesus, at least tacitly, acknowledged his kingship. A principal charge, exacerbated by the hosannas and the entrance on a donkey, was Jesus' alleged prediction that the Temple would be destroyed or, according to some accusers, that he would destroy it. His accusers disagreed as to what precisely he said. He probably, and correctly, predicted that the Temple would soon be destroyed – relating its demise to himself, the new temple, the place where heaven and earth meet. It is worth mentioning that, in the ancient world, and still often today, biodiversity surrounds temples, and some monasteries, with flowers, trees, fruit, and wildlife, a symbolic extension of the temple, God's presence, as the place of harmony and shalom, of all redeemed creatures.

What Jesus does not say, or respond, at his trials is significant – and his human creatures, now his judges, knew it. 'He was silent and made no answer', says Mark (Mk 14:61). 'He gave him no answer, not even to a single charge', adds Matthew (Mt 27:12-14). Herod, says Luke, questioned Jesus at some length, 'but he made no answer' (Lk 23:9). In John's almost dramatic trial scene, Pilate, shaken by Jesus' silence, bursts out, 'You will not speak to me? Do you not know that I have power to release you, and power to crucify you?' (Jn 19:10). There are rich springs awaiting discovery in the silent depths of scripture. We are invited to discover, and ponder, the relationship of Jesus' cosmic kingship, to which his silence attests, to other ways, other religions, and to the inclusion of the earth in our redemption, and our future. The salvation ecology in the depths of Jesus' silence at his trials is one of the concealed wonders in the New Testament, described by John Henry Newman:

> It cannot, as it were, be mapped, or its contents catalogued;
> but after all our diligence, to the end of our lives and to the

end of the church, it must be an unexplored and unsubdued land, with heights and valleys, forests and streams, on the right and left of our path and close about us, full of concealed wonders and choice treasures.[5]

The Potters' Field

Judas accepted money for betraying Jesus. But he did not spend or keep it. Judas threw the silver back at the Jewish leaders' feet. They purchased a field with it, probably in south-east Jerusalem, where the Hinnom and Kidron valleys meet. Temple servants poured used water, often mixed with sacrificial lambs' blood, onto the potters' field, hence its alternative name, Haceldema, 'the field of blood'. There is poignant coincidence between the blood of sacrificial lambs poured onto the soil of Haceldema, and the blood of the Lamb of God poured out for many. We have especial reverence for Jesus' blood: the 'cup of my blood' at the Last Supper, and in our eucharists; the blood, sweat at Gethsemane; the blood at the praetorium scourgings; and his blood, and water, flowing onto the soil beneath the cross at Golgotha. We commemorate these mysteries in our worship, and theological art, and in feasts of the Precious Blood. We may also include, within salvation ecology, Haceldema, the field of blood, which is forever associated with temple lambs and with Judas. Judas, even more than the impulsive Peter, is a problem for us, for Judas betrayed not only Jesus but all of us who identify with Jesus. Dante is hard on Judas, relegating him to 'the lowest and the darkest and the farthest from the sphere that circles all' (The Inferno, ix, 128). But let us recall that naked youth fleeing through the olives. Others betray Jesus too, in myriad ways, not least by abuse of the fields, animals, plants, and the climate which he redeemed. To repeat John Zizioulas, 'to hurt the earth is a sin'. Everyone needs forgiveness. Even 'the lowest, darkest, and farthest' is within reach of the embrace of the cosmic cross.

The Skull

With Pilate's cynical hand washing, which again includes water

in the life, and now the death, of the Messiah, Jesus' final walk,
to Golgotha, begins. The soldiers impressed Simon, a Cyrenian
gardener, coming from the fields *(ap agrou)* to carry Jesus' cross
beam to Golgotha. Luke notes that Simon walked after Jesus
(opisthen tou Jesu), possibly a hint that Simon, with his sons
Alexander and Rufus, was, or soon became, a disciple (Lk 23:27).
Simon is forever special among farmers, rural people, and food
gardeners who follow Jesus. Perhaps we should notice Simon
more. Perhaps Simon should be a patron of the rural church, of
country parishes, of those who love the countryside, of gardeners, and of allotments. Simon disappears from the Bible almost
as soon as we meet him and his sons. But we have never forgotten Simon, who worked the fields, and carried the cross behind
Jesus. He is the fifth of our 14 'stations' of the cross, adorning the
walls of our churches where, especially in Lent, we commemorate Jesus' passion. Sometimes, as in Eric Gill's fifth station at
Westminster Cathedral, some weeping women, like Simon and
his sons, walked with Jesus in his torment, and sympathised.
Jesus also comforted *them* (Lk 28:27-31, 39). To this day, other
women throughout the earth, including communities of religious sisters, spend hours in chapels in Holy Week, with Simon
and the Jerusalem women, sympathising, which means co-suf-
fering, with Jesus on his way of the cross.

Golgotha was a rocky, skull shaped mound, just outside the
city, which later was within, when Herod Agrippa enlarged
Jerusalem with another wall. Golgotha had been a quarry, a place
of tombs, and a garden, curiously similar to some former quar-
ries today. Cyril of Jerusalem, ordained shortly after
Constantine's basilica was dedicated, said of Golgotha, 'It was a
garden where he was crucified. For though it has been extensive-
ly decorated with royal gifts, it was once a garden, and the signs
and remains of it still exist.'[6] The cross, fastened in Golgotha
stone, pointed to the heavens above the heavens, and the mountain behind the mountain. Irenaeus of Lyons, recalling the letter
to the Ephesians' exultation in the height and depth and length
and breadth of Jesus' love, describes the cosmic cross:

He extends his influence in the world through its (whole) length, breadth, height and depth. For, by the Word of God, all things are subject to the influence of the economy of redemption, and the Son of God has been crucified for all, having traced the sign of the cross on all things. For it was right and necessary that he who made himself visible should lead all visible things to participate in his cross; and it is in this way that, in a form that can be perceived, his own special influence has had its sensible effect on visible things: for it is he that illumines the heights, that is the heavens; it is he that penetrates that which is beneath; he that traverses the whole vast extent from east to west, and he that covers the immense distance from north to south, summoning to the knowledge of his Father those scattered in every place. (*Demonstratio* 34)

Here at Golgotha is the centre of the earth, of history, and of the cosmos. Jesus' suffering and slow death, between earth and heaven, in the untimely shadows, was, and is, the beginning of the closing of the cosmic circle of redemption. Cyril of Jerusalem writes, 'He stretched out his arms on the cross that he might embrace the ends of the world. For this Golgotha is the very centre of the earth ... He stretched forth human hands who by his spiritual hands had established the heavens.'[7] Christian art, at its imaginative finest and deepest, sometimes depicts this cosmic act – and its connection with creation and history – by portraying the crucifixion from above, with the blood from our Saviour's wounds cleansing the earth, and Adam's skull beneath the cosmic cross.

Two convicts were crucified with Jesus. Possibly they were brigands, perhaps robbers, highwaymen, zealot insurgents, or proto-terrorists. Perhaps they were gentiles. Of the three Jesus became the most remembered person in history. The others are almost forgotten. But not quite. One, whom tradition remembers as Dismas, sympathised with Jesus, and believed in him. We have not forgotten Dismas. Unlike the other crucified convict, and the freed Barabbas, we sometimes sense his presence among us, especially during Holy Week triduum. Prisoners –

and prison chapels – honour him. A prison chaplain I have known took his name. Jesus assured Dismas he would 'this day' be with him in paradise, a word borrowed from the Iranian *pairi-daeza*. In 401 BC the Greek historian Xenophon, moved by the blossoms, fragrance, shade, and beautifully coloured fruit of a Persian walled garden, designed his own on his Greek estate, and introduced a new word into Greek. The transliteration of the Persian *pairidaeza*, became the Latin *paradeisos*, and our word, and image, *paradise*. Our green and golden quince trees, a late arrival in Britain, join us from north Persia, a fragrant reminder of Jesus' words to the penitent convict we remember as Dismas. Jesus' compassion towards the compassionate Dismas is continuous with his compassion throughout that shattering day: the healed ear, the forgiven Peter, the weeping women and their children, Dismas – Calvary is an epicentre of mercy, cosmic and very, very small.

The gospels report uncanny darkness as Jesus dies. Matthew goes further – as darkness falls, the earth quakes, rocks split, graves open, the dead arise, the Temple veil is torn, the nameless centurion exclaims, 'Truly this was the Son of God' (Mt 27:41-54). More than portents of judgement, these earthly signs show cosmic compassion, creation co-suffers, the earth shudders at the death of creation's King. An Afro-American hymn asks, 'Were you there when the sun refused to shine?'

Since the day at Golgotha, for Christians trees symbolise the cross. For the first Jewish Christians, a plough in a field, a sailing ship at sea, an upright man, and every tree recalled the cross. Irenaeus of Asia Minor and Lyons, in the second century, includes the Golgotha tree that was the cross in the restoring of history and ecology, in the New Adam. 'He became obedient unto death, even the death of the cross, rectifying that disobedience which had occurred by reason of a tree, through the obedience wrought upon the tree.'[8] In the beautiful sixth-century *Pange Lingua*, which we still sing in Holy Week, God selects the tree that became the cross: 'himself at that very time marked out the tree which should make good the loss caused by the Tree'. In

another exquisite early poem, *The Dream of the Rood*, an anony-
mous bystander hears the cross itself speaking words of cosmic
involvement, even sympathy, at the death of 'the Ruler':

> They mocked us together. I was soaked in the blood
> streaming from the man's side after he set his spirit free.
> I underwent many horrors on that hill.
> I saw the God of hosts stretched on the rack.
> Clouds of darkness gathered over the corpse
> of the Ruler; and shadows, black shapes
> under the clouds, swept across
> his shining splendour. All creation wept,
> wailed at the king's death. Christ was on the cross.
> *(The Dream of the Rood)*

In John's gospel, the nameless soldier pierced Jesus' side with a
lance, opening his human heart, from which blood and water
flow onto the earth, of which he, God's Word infleshed, is a part.
In this favourite biblical scene, blood and water, a symbol of
self-emptying, with many connotations, flow onto the earth
community, onto Adam beneath the cross, and onto all his descendants, the precious blood and water mingling with the cosmic Jordan, salvation ecology at its most memorable. A member
of John's community later combined the Jordan with Jesus'
blood: 'Not with the water only, but with the water and the
blood' (1 Jn 5:6). So did Bishop Ignatius, of Antioch: 'He was
born and baptised that he might sanctify the waters by his passion' (Eph 18:2). Artists and poets celebrate salvation ecology in
Jesus' blood and water, associating the open side with the
woman at the cross, the New Eve, the bones of Adam beneath,
the beloved disciple, the water of baptism, the blood of the eucharist, new creation, a new garden. The cosmic cross, at the centre of the cosmos, bearing the first born of all creation, reconciles
all creation, seen and unseen, all that God has made, all the elements of 14 billion years of evolution of life, animals, and plants,
all the deepest aspirations from the first primate hearts to the
outermost star. In his body Jesus contains all the elements of the
universe. An eleventh-century Celtic writing, *The Evernew*

Tongue Here Below, celebrates Jesus the microcosm, in whose fullness all creation is held:

> Every material and every element and every nature which is seen in the world were all combined in the body in which Christ arose, that is in the body of every human person ... All the world arose with him, for the nature of all the elements was in the body which Jesus assumed.[9]

In Golgotha, says John, 'there was a garden', and in the garden a new tomb, there tenderly wrapped in elements of the earth, accompanied by Joseph of Arimathea and Nicodemus, Jesus' body rested at last, in the rocks of the earth. Darkness descended. It was night. And the ring of dawn of a new creation.

Descent, Ascent, Filling All

The cosmic cross, the cosmic circle, in their fullness, surround and embrace believers and unbelievers alike, and all the creatures of the cosmos. Teilhard de Chardin, moved by Jesus' cosmic fullness, exclaimed, 'I love you as a world, as the world which has captured my heart, and it is you, I now realise, whom men and women, my brothers and sisters, even those who do not believe, serve and seek throughout the magic immensities of the cosmos.'[10] In his fullness, his 'pleroma', Jesus fills the stars, the whole evolution of the earth, history past, present, and future, all 'the good dead in the green hills', and the ashes, and stars of yesteryear. In his descent into death, Jesus entered, and redeemed, even death which, as Von Baltasar said, 'is not a partial event' but, rather, as Shakespeare wrote, 'The undiscovered country, from whose bourn no traveller returns'. The former 'descents' of incarnation, and the Jordan, reach forward to the descent into death. Kilian McDonnell writes:

> The Jordan descensus ruptures the space-time bonds, proclaiming that the power of Christ transforms those living in the present, grasps those still in the far reaches of the future, but, triumph of triumph, overthrows sequence and succession to enter the past, there to bring the good news not as a hope but as a realised salvation. The Lord of the Cosmos, the Sovereign of the Universe, claims his universal dominion.[11]

The descent is really threefold, into the earth community, into the river and, finally, into death, which is not a partial event. St Paul, our earliest writer, relates the descent to Jesus' *ascent*, 'far above all the heavens, where he fills all things' (Eph 4:4; cf Rom 10:6-7). Through his descent, and ascent, Jesus fills the whole evolving cosmos with 'the breadth and length, and height, and depth' of God's love for his human creatures, and for all 'the magic immensities of the cosmos'. Lionel Swain writes beautifully:

> His descent into Sheol also has a cosmic significance. Sheol is, after all, part of creation – the antipodes of heaven. By passing, actively, from Sheol into heaven, Jesus has made his presence felt in the whole of the cosmos. Nowhere, no created thing, is outside the sphere of his all-embracing influence. His descent into the nether recesses of the cosmos, followed by his ascension 'far above all the heavens' is part of the process by which he fills 'all things' (Eph 4:9-10).[12]

With his triple descent, and his ascent, Jesus completes the cosmic circle: from incarnation, the Nazareth years, the wilderness and cosmic Jordan, the public ministry, and the death, triumph, and ascent, far above all the heavens, filling 'all things' – and God is all, in all.

After the Cross

The cross is now a sign of triumph, and of contradiction, 'the great sign of Christ's strength and power', said Justin Martyr, in the second century (*First Apology*, 55).[13] The events after Jesus' death, and after his burial in the garden, are as astonishing to ourselves as they were to our brethren, the first Christians. Even in a post-Christian, post-modernist age, I am struck every time we profess our faith visibly and audibly at Easter, when the veils come off, the bells ring, and the early spring sun rises promisingly in the east. Bishop Tom Wright well describes our astonishment, when he says of our earliest brethren, to whom, after God, we owe the gospels, that they experienced 'an event for which there was no precedent and of which there remains as yet no subsequent example, an event involving neither the resuscitation nor the abandonment of a physical body, but its transformation into a new mode of physicality.'[14]

Paul reports actual appearances of Jesus, transformed, but in continuity with the Jesus of Galilee and Judea. In his public ministry, we noted the communal meals, inaugurating the kingdom on earth, with disciples around Jesus breaking bread and serving food. At Emmaus, Cleopas and his companion recognise the same Jesus, risen but the same, breaking bread at table. Caravaggio and later Velasquez capture that instant of recognition – as Adam and Eve's 'eyes were opened' in Eden, so were the two disciples' at Emmaus, in the new Eden, new creation, the eighth day. There is both continuity, the same Jesus, and discontinuity: as at Tabor God's glory shines through. In Dominic Milroy OSB's words, 'He is both profoundly different, and profoundly the same.' The same Jesus, risen and transformed, just as in our future we will be profoundly the same, yet risen and transformed in him. We exist 'in Christ' now, in physical bodies animated by human souls. As risen, we will exist in those same bodies, profoundly different because animated by God's Spirit. The late, revered New Testament scholar, George Caird, said, 'In Christ is already seen the full character of God, and that fullness is now being imparted to the church as the first decisive step in the process by which it is to be imparted to the universe.'[15] Heaven, therefore, is not above and apart, but includes the universe. John McDade SJ, writes, 'In heaven our condition will be different but it will still be our condition and therefore the self will have in heaven an embodied expressiveness. Souls need bodies because only in that way can they be personal and social; only as embodied souls can we love "now" and "then".'[16] McDade could have added that only as embodied can we be 'personal and social and earth beings', only as embodied are we, in the embodied and risen Jesus, within the earth, and universe, community. Matter matters, to ourselves, as to God.

The Liturgy

The gospels relate Jesus' resurrection to sunrise. He, and no nature god, is, in Melito's fine phrase, 'the sun out of heaven'. Mark concludes with an appendix, describing resurrection appearances. Mark's Jesus tells his disciples to 'Go into all the world and preach the gospel to the whole creation' (Mk 16:15). In our globalised, urban, almost disembodied culture, Bible scholars hesitate to affirm that Jesus' commission means just what it says – 'preach the gospel to the whole creation'. They acknowledge that the word *ktisis* elsewhere in Mark means material creation, as it does in Paul's famous hymn in Romans 8:19-23, where all material creation groans and waits our revelation as God's sons. But exegetes hesitate to say that Mark's Jesus means what he says in commissioning the disciples (and all of us) to preach the gospel to all creatures. Francis of Assisi, in his intuitive grasp of the gospel, was less hesitant: his famous sermon to the birds at Bevagna began a regular practice: 'From that day on, he solicitously admonished all birds, all animals, and reptiles, and even creatures that have no feeling, to praise and love their Creator, for daily, when the name of the Saviour had been invoked, he saw their obedience by personal experience.'[17] The French theologian, Jean Bastaire, agrees: 'It is time Christians had recourse to the plenitude of the gospel, to announce the good news not only to all the nations, but as St Mark says, to the whole creation.'[18] In the Holy Saturday *Exultet*, it seems to me, we do what the Marcan Jesus tells us to do – we liturgise, evangelise, tell to rejoice, all creatures, visible and invisible, whom God has made. Perhaps we should sing the *Exultet* more often:

Rejoice, heavenly powers! Sing, choirs of angels!
Exult, all creation around God's throne!
Jesus Christ, our King, is risen!
Sound the trumpet of salvation!
Rejoice, O earth, in shining splendour,
Radiant in the brightness of your King!
Christ has conquered! Glory fills you!
Darkness vanishes for ever!

Rejoice, O Mother Church! Exult in glory!
The risen Saviour shines upon you!
Let this place resound with joy,
Echoing the mighty song of all God's people!

In preaching the gospel, I suggest we should remain open to inarticulate depths within the eyes of other sensate creatures, something beyond the sensate, more than material, something 'far more deeply interfused', akin to what Noel Dermot O'Donoghue calls 'the physical incorruptible'. As Metropolitan John of Pergamon notices, 'Consciousness, even self-consciousness, is to be found in animals too, the difference between them and man being one of degree not of kind.'[19] I can see connections clicking in my peke's eyes, when she sees certain clothes appear, at certain times of day, signifying a spell in the garden, or a walk; or when luggage appears at the door, threatening separation, and she stations herself anxiously at the door. I also know that when my territorial robin sits next to me – and he sits very close and trusting indeed – during winter digging in our shared garden, pestering me to produce a worm, snatching that priceless creature promptly when I do, I sometimes scold back. I ask my robin kindly to develop a craving for hooligan slugs of unknown parents. I suspect other organic growers communicate similarly. If we get that far in addressing other earth creatures, which is still not as far as our *Exultet* goes, why cannot we tell them about salvation ecology in Jesus? Sometimes, in fact, with the compiler of that Marcan appendix, and with Francis of Assisi, I do. New creation – paradise – would be lonely without peke companions, and transfigured garden robins.

John's gospel, like Mark, also concludes with an appendix. The author, or redactor, of that final chapter tells us that Mary Magdalen was the first to visit the garden tomb, 'when it was still dark', just before the ring of dawn of the Eighth Day. She meets Jesus risen, walking in the garden, like God in Eden, 'profoundly the same and profoundly different'. Mary's initially mistaking Jesus for the gardener is profound irony with many connotations. Jesus in fact is the Gardener, the New Adam, as the open side on the cross intimates, Master of garden earth, the One in whom, with whom, and under whom all human gardeners garden. Yet he is the same Jesus who walked in Galilee, profoundly the same, continuity in discontinuity, with all God's glory shining through. Mary recognises him in his use of her name. Later, in the upper room the doubting Thomas is invited to put his hand in Jesus' side, the same opened side, the same Jesus of Nazareth, and of Galilee, the new Adam, with God's glory shining through. John's gospel, which began near Jordan's living waters, which includes Cana and Jacob's well, the Lake, the pool of Bethesda, the foot washing, and the pierced side from which blood and living water flow, concludes with Jesus preparing and sharing a meal at the Lake. There, where the cosmic Jordan flows, in that numinous place of water and fertility, as the small boats come home from the night, Jesus confirms Peter, the forgiven fisherman, shepherd of the flock (Jn 21:15-17).

The varied writings of John's community, which began with Jesus, recognised by the Baptist as 'the Lamb of God', conclude with the Lamb enthroned, from whom a living river flows with the fruiting tree of life and its leaves which heal the nations.

We demonstrate our hope in the Lamb's return, in the way we live and walk our talk, as the rural Irish, until recently, literally did, when they walked through the fields to Mass. Our preaching, we have suggested, should include fellowship meals, the breaking of bread together in small local groups, and love of all our neighbours, including all the earth's soil and water creatures. Whenever two or three – or more – gather in his name, he is there in our midst. Our preaching, our walking, includes support of all efforts towards local sustainable sufficiency. When those who notice our deeds and words begin to say, 'See how they love one another, and their neighbours – and the earth', we are being heard, we are effective signs, or sacraments, of the Lamb's return.

Notes:
1. Paul Evdokimov, *The Art of the Icon: A Theology of Beauty*, (Redondo Beach: Oakwood Publications, 1990), p. 117.
2. Richard Baukham and Trevor Hart, *At the Cross* (London: Darton, Longman & Todd, 1999), p. 120.
3. Pliny the Elder, *Natural History, A Selection* (London: Penguin Books, 1991), p. 197.
4. Jonathan Gorsky, 'Rabbis in Conflict', *Common Ground*, 1 (2002), p. 12; cf. Deut 20:19.
5. John Henry Newman, *An Essay on the Development of Christian Doctrine* (London: Longman Green, 1909), p. 71.
6. Cyril of Jerusalem, Lecture XIV, *The Nicene and Post-Nicene Fathers, Vol. VII, Cyril of Jerusalem and Gregory Nazianzen*, Philip Schaff and Henry Wace, eds. (Edinburgh: T. &T. Clark, 1989), p. 95.
7. Cyril of Jerusalem, Lecture XIII, Ibid., p. 93.
8. Irenaeus, 'Against Heresies', V, 16, *The Anti-Nicene Fathers, Vol. 1, The Apostolic Fathers*, p. 544.
9. *Celts and Christians*, Mark Atherton, ed. (Cardiff: University of Wales Press, 2002), p. 188.
10. In Wendy M. Wright, *Sacred Heart: Gateway to God* (London: Darton, Longman & Todd, 2002), p. 22.
11. McDonnell, *The Baptism of Jesus*, p. 170.
12. Lionel Swain, 'Descent of Christ into Hell', *The New Dictionary of Theology*, Joseph A. Komonchak, Mary Collins, Dermot A. Lane, eds. (Dublin: Gill & Macmillan, 1987), p. 280.
13. Justin Martyr, 'The First Apology', 55, *The Ante-Nicene Fathers, Vol. 1*, p. 181.
14. N. T. Wright, *The Challenge of Jesus* (London: SPCK, 2000), pp. 110-111.
15. G. B. Caird, *Paul's Letters from Prison* (Oxford: OUP, 1976), p. 43.
16. John McDade SJ, 'Heaven, Then and Now', *New Blackfriars* (January 2002) p. 44.
17. Thomas of Celano, 'First Life of St Francis', 58, in *St Francis of Assisi: Writings and Early Biographies: English Omnibus of the Sources for the Life of St Francis*, M.A. Habig, ed. (Quincy: Franciscan Press, 1991), p. 278.
18. Jean Bastaire, 'Une Affirmation Chrètienne Fondamentale: La Dimension Cosmique Du Salut' (Paris: 2001), unpublished leaflet.
19. John Zizioulas, 'Preserving God's Creation, I', *King's Theological Review*, 12 (1989), p. 3.

CHAPTER SEVEN

Liturgising the Plough

We belong to the land.
And the land we belong to is grand.
(Oklahoma)

'What', it will be questioned, 'when the sun rises do you not see
a round disc of fire somewhat like a guinea?' 'Oh no, no I see an
innumerable company of the heavenly host crying,
"Holy, holy, holy is the Lord God Almighty".'
(William Blake)

Our time is one of rapid change. So rapid that when we think of
our parents' world, we say 'The past is a foreign country. They
do things differently there.' After World War II, and before the
Second Vatican Council, I grew up in a technologically heady
age, epitomised by the slogan, 'America is the place where you
have no story but the story you made when you had no story.'
Having triumphed twice 'over there', and humbled the Rising
Sun, we were the chosen ones, with a 'manifest destiny' to conquer a continent. Our response to new challenges was 'can do'.
At the University of Detroit High School, 'Cubs' was our logo.
The new Air Force Academy, in the Colorado Rockies, took as
its motto, 'Give us men to match these mountains.' We chaffed,
and pawed the ground, eager to finish school, to go out and
match those mountains, to make our stories. When we graduated
'go Cubs' was our cry. But there was another side. Fortunately
for the mountains, and for ourselves, our teachers told us, especially in their lives, which were the tacit curriculum, that the real
story is God's story. Our annual retreats, especially the words of
Christ in the kingdom meditation, taught us where to find the
real mountain: 'Whoever wishes to come with me must labour
with me, so that following me in pain, he may likewise follow
me in glory.' The mountains were there alright but the real chal-

lenges were the Sinai, the Mount of Olives, Golgotha, the New Jerusalem. So with difficulty we did not completely buy into our age. As Chesterton said, 'It is easy to let the age have its head. The difficult thing is to keep one's own.'

Salvation Ecology in Jesus

God's story is salvation history, including salvation ecology, in Jesus. From the very origins and depths of the 'Bang', God enables the whole evolution of our cosmos, the whole cosmogenesis. Some four billion years ago our planet earth formed, culminating, after the demise of the dinosaurs, in our lush, fertile, biodiverse age, in which the living earth, in our humanity, stands up and consciously begins to pray. Salvation history, and ecology, climaxes when, in Jesus, God opens human arms on the cosmic cross embracing our whole living, conscious, and praying planet. In Jesus, we behold 'the breadth, and length and height and depth, and ... know the love of Christ which surpasses knowledge' (Eph 3:18-19). The whole cosmic community bows, implicitly or explicitly, to God in Jesus: 'Every knee should bow, in heaven and on earth and under the earth, and every tongue confess that Jesus Christ is Lord, to the glory of God the Father' (Phil 2:10-11). As our beautiful, fragile earth, after four billion years of evolution, falters and fails under unsustainable human numbers and impact, I believe more people, already now and in the imminent future, will listen to the Jesus story.

The Earth's Hunger

During my doctoral studies in ecumenical theology at Ottawa University, there were some Jesuit colleagues doing doctoral studies in psychology. A popular writer and dissertation favourite of the time was the Austrian psychologist, Erich Fromm. Fromm was, and still is, associated with human love which he described as an art. Less well known is Fromm's assessment of modern, perhaps we should say post-modern, people, whom Fromm calls 'non-people', unable to love, because of dysfunctional relationships with the earth, other people, and the future:

Man, in the name of progress, is transforming the world into a stinking and poisonous place (and this is not symbolic). He pollutes the air, the water, the soil, the animals – and himself. He is doing this to a degree that has made it doubtful whether the earth will still be liveable within a hundred years from now. He knows the facts, but in spite of many protesters, those in charge go on in the pursuit of technical 'progress' and are willing to sacrifice all life in the worship of their idol. In earlier times men also sacrificed their children or war prisoners, but never before in history has man been willing to sacrifice all life to the Moloch – his own and that of all his descendants.[1]

Fromm's piercing, readily recognisable analysis surprises only because of the man from whom it comes, whom we associate with 'love is an art', and 'the art of loving'. We need the art of earth reverence, and love, if Fromm's prognosis, strikingly similar to that of conservation biologists and environmentalists, is to be revised. For people committed to inexhaustible, indiscriminate love, in Jesus, our Creator within his creation, indiscriminate love of the earth community flows from that commitment. Love includes love of all that the beloved loves. The art of loving God, present in the earth, is Christian ecology – in practice. All things near and far are loved, and redeemed, in Jesus. The art of earth loving begins locally, with our immediate neighbours, our own habitats, our garden, fig tree, and vine.

Some argue that the Jesus love story, at least as told by academic theologians, is no longer relevant in the gardens of the west. Theological publisher, Alex Wright, claims that the Jesus movement has lost young people from seventeen to thirty-five:

Our postmodern world, with all its glittering opportunities, its freedoms of choice, its openings, can so easily become a prison if it lacks love or understanding or wisdom. It is the drive towards these, and the vacuum traditional theological teaching has left behind, that have prompted many people in our society to look elsewhere.[2]

I agree that much so-called theology is irrelevant, as theology conferences repeatedly demonstrate. I would go further, and add that preaching too, when almost delimited to anecdotes and illustrations, leaves genuine seekers who occasionally 'drop in' or accompany relatives to our services, as well as 'regular' worshippers, unimpressed. Where I differ from Wright, and also from new agers who insist they can 'do it better' with a pick-and-mix spiritual Round Up Ready, is in the principle that *abusum non tollit usum*, that is, too many Christians' refusal to teach and live what God does for the whole earth community in Jesus does not mean we should abandon God and Jesus. Christian love of the earth because Jesus, incarnate and risen, loves, and is at the very centre of the earth, is the distinct Christian contribution to healing the non-persons whom Erich Fromm describes, and to healing the earth community which they damage.

The Wow of the Market
At the public inquiry about a La Farge Redland proposal to fasten a super-quarry on the Hebridean island of Lewis, Free Church theologian and pastor, Dr Donald Macleod, spoke for conservationists, concluding:

> Do we have God's mandate to inflict on Creation a scar of this magnitude that might detract from Creation's ability to reflect the glory of God? I know that Roineabhal is not in itself an area of what you might deem to be 'beautiful'. It is nevertheless an area of magnificence and grandeur and, by being such, bears eloquent testimony in my judgement to the majesty and grandeur of God's Earth. In my view no hole in the ground could bear that testimony as Roineabhal presently does.[3]

Macleod's exposition of the Christian contribution was as brilliant as his conclusion is unassailable. The proposal was not carried. The reaction of the charismatic leader of the Hebridean conservationists, Alastair McIntosh, approximates that of environmentalists I have known, when they discover the meaning of salvation ecology in Jesus, that in Jesus God walked the earth and, as risen, fills the earth now. By letting be the rocky green island of Lewis, the conservationists let God's glory through. 'His testimony was gripping', said McIntosh. 'It was the sort of thing that makes you think, "Wow! If that's what Christianity's about, then I'm all for it".' Whether we are Christians born and bred, or converts to 'the Way', or just plain seekers who care about the earth, there is scarce need to seek earth love and light in pick-and-mixes. What we who are Christians have to do, with our sympathisers, is to let all God's glory through the islands, mountains, and riverine cities where we live. Holy Mystery is present, immanent within the earth, loving the earth in Jesus. We need to rediscover the inexhaustible depths of our own green heritage, articulate them as did Donald Macleod, and share our heritage with the contemporary culture Erich Fromm describes. That sharing, preaching, evangelisation, teaching begins by walking our talk, sometimes literally. To paraphrase St Francis, preach – and teach our youngsters sustainable sufficiency always, sometimes use words. Ghandi put the same undeniable wisdom this way: 'We must become the change we want to see.'

People notice, and worry about, the increasing earth illiteracy of young people, who know more about computers than carrots, who believe food originates in supermarkets, and who know not the connection between chickens and eggs. Mike Russell of Sussex Wildlife Trust says, 'There is now a concern arising as to where the next generation of naturalists will come from. Young people don't necessarily have access to the countryside, as perhaps once was the case.' Like ourselves, who should be informing and sensitising them, children are unaware of the ominous significance of the fact that London imports over half its vegetables and a shocking and expensive 95 per cent of its fruit, mostly by air and lorry, contributing enormously and unsustainably to food miles, climate disruption, asthma, chemical agribusiness, and fossil fuel dependence.[4] According to Sustain, London itself could supply one of the five green portions we need daily. London, like Heathrow, in stone, iron, and saner ages, was a fruit and vegetable paradise. Look at my own Williams Bon Chrètien (Bartlett) pear cordon – and all those Merton apple varieties. In addition to apples, pears, figs, grapes, medlars, mulberries, plums, damsons, and cultivated cherries, the Romans imported vegetable biodiversity to southern Britain. Jane Renfrew writes, 'They grew peas and beans and imported lentils into Britain. They introduced a number of vegetable crops such as cabbage, onion, leek, shallots, carrots, endive, globe artichokes, cucumber, marrow, asparagus, parsnip, turnip, radish and celery. They also ate a number of wild plants.'[5] Expanding population, migrations, construction on agricultural land, including fields cultivated by Romans and their predecessors, with massive food imports, make the continuation of human life, on this crowded island, plane and fossil fuel dependent. Fossil fuel dependence is our Lumpers potato monocrop of the present, our 'great hunger' certain to happen. We rarely teach youngsters, at home, school, or church, or in our neighbourhoods, to engage in fruit and vegetable growing. Our county wildlife trusts and NGOs struggle to attract young members. Britain imports not only tons of organic food but also doctors and nurses. Too often education at home, schools, and tertiary 'Unis' prepares youngsters only for 'getting ahead', 'choice', and life within the market culture, which to many contemporaries is a virtual deity. Harvey Cox writes perceptively:

All of the traditional religions teach that human beings are finite creatures and that there are limits to any earthly enterprise. A Japanese Zen master once said to his disciples as he was dying, 'I have learned only one thing in life: how much is enough.' He would find no niche in the chapel of The Market, for whom the First Commandment is 'There is never enough'. Like the proverbial shark that stops moving, The Market that stops expanding dies. That could happen. If it does, then Nietzsche will have been right after all. He will just have had the wrong God in mind.[6]

How Begin?

As seas rise, summers warm, and flooding recurs, while politicians nevertheless build more roads and runways, and holiday in Barbados, where – and how – do we begin to heal, and regenerate, the earth? The responses to this persistent, probing, deceptively profound question, which challenges each of us, are both as simple, and as challenging, as when Fritz Schumacher addressed it in the sixties. The response to the 'where?' is brief. The 'where' to begin is with number one, ourselves, that's you and me. The 'how?' likewise has a brief, but also a long response. The brief response which, perhaps, we should stick onto our mirrors is – live sustainably locally. That's the short response to the 'how?' – local sustainability – in developed and 'developing' regions. The longer response to the 'how?' will engage us for the remainder of this book.

All of us, whatever our neighbourhood, garden, age, health, or mobility, can begin today by what we have called 'liturgising the cosmos'. That mouthful, once it's unpacked, is neither esoteric nor threatening. The American Catholic Bishops, in their letter on climate, quoted Pope John Paul II's reference to cosmic liturgy: 'Respect for life and for the dignity of the human person extends also to the rest of creation, which is called to join man in praising God.'[7] Liturgising the cosmos means bringing to our worship, especially the eucharist, all that God has made and saved; or, put another way, it means letting all creatures pray with us, as they do in the Psalms, letting the cosmos, visible and invisible, bring itself to our worship. We do just that when we pray the Psalms, and in some prefaces to our *Sanctus*, and in the *Sanctus* itself. In our eucharists we recognise that all creation, visible and invisible, the whole universe, is transformed by the incarnation, and redemption in Jesus. Cardinal Avery Dulles SJ notes, 'Jesus has an importance far beyond the community of the disciples and even beyond the whole of humanity. His existence and career have constitutive and transformative importance for the entire universe, including both the material and the spiritual realms.'[8] We recognise Jesus' importance 'for the entire universe' when we welcome the angels, animals, birds, trees, and plants to our worship. They are already there in our medieval churches, in the wood, stone, glass, and cloth.

Our services already are a cosmic liturgy, as in the *Sanctus*, and in the Holy Saturday 'Festival of Lights'. Liturgising the cosmos, including all creatures in our prayers, spills over into our daily lives. With the world rapidly urbanising, we need imaginative creativity in integrating the natural world with the built environment. Even picking up a piece of litter, which another has discarded, reverses slightly the defacement of our locality, and becomes part of our worship. More satisfying, because more leafy, visible, and permanent, is restoring and pruning neglected trees or plants which have been vandalised or just left friendless. Most satisfying of all is planting anew, adding a new living member to our community. Nothing we do to heal, restore, regenerate, or replant is wasted. Even our failures are included in our worship. We Christians are here to make sacraments throughout the earth, both to succeed and to fail, to plant trees and heal what is abused, to replenish the earth with fruit and beauty, to let wildlife habitats complement the built environment, to grow food even in cities, to let the cosmic Christ shine through the earth – in brief, to liturgise the cosmos. Letting Christ's glory through the earth is, or includes, evangelisation. Being Christ today is our lifestyle, telling people, in words and practice, what God did and does for the universe in Jesus. We bring good news about the inexhaustible 'breadth and length and height and depth' of God's love. We radiate the *Exultet* even when we don't use words. We can make a significant contribution to the earth community by teaching our youngsters about the beauty, needs, and fragility of the earth, and by asking them to accompany us in evangelisation. Their special contribution is in evangelising other youth – and some not so young – telling them about creation, incarnation, and redemption, in the young Christ.

The Angels' Ancient Places

I want to include here a word about the 'physical incorruptible' presences, who pray with us in our locality. With my limited ability to fathom, let alone describe, our power of intimation, I can only mention the presences around us who share our cosmic liturgy. Look again at our services and prayers – we just mentioned the *Sanctus* – continuous with centuries of Christian prayer with fellow creatures. Look more closely at Psalm 148, and at the *Exultet;* listen to the presences in the prefaces to our eucharists; recall again the prayers some of us once said, and perhaps still do, to guardian angels; consider the location of so many Irish and British churches at sacred springs, wells, and rivers; look again, and often, at the carvings the medieval craftsmen left behind in our ancient churches. Most of us have our favourites. I am struck by the Borromeo Chapel at Ushaw College, the angel choir at Lincoln, the misericords in many ancient churches, the bench ends in East Anglia; the animals are there too, as at Earl Soham church in Suffolk, and Hugh of Lincoln's swan at Lincoln. Whenever I enter St Aloysius, formerly the Jesuit church, now the Oratory, at Oxford, I am reminded that we glorify God in a communion of visible and invisible presences. The chancel walls are, literally, encircled by stone carvings of the good dead, mysteriously still present with us. I preached at St Aloysius once, when a doctoral student at Campion Hall, and felt overwhelmed because Gerard Manley Hopkins was once a curate there, and preached from that same pulpit. Hopkins knew something about the real but invisible: his most famous line is 'The world is charged with the grandeur of God.' John Henry Newman preached there too, as have many others, Jesuits and Oratorians, who, though deceased, are present. This, of course, is true of all churches and chapels. I'm just unusually reminded of 'the communion of saints' at St Aloysius.

How then can we bring the cosmos, all things created, visible and invisible, to our worship? How can we let the earth enter our services? What tangibly, and locally, can we do to worship more cosmically, more greenly, letting God's grandeur 'flame out like shining from shook foil'? Big questions these, to which I propose just a few initial suggestions. For once we get our worship right, our prayer will flow into practice – beckoning more young adults and children to join us in prayer, and in earth care. The brilliantly imaginative Sisters, still around in Britain and Ireland and America, with their flair for holistic worship, can lead us, as they do when asked at conferences. For starters let's welcome the angels back. They're already there in the *Sanctus*, and in medieval carvings, and they're a corrective to earth exclusive anthroposolism. They're present even in our Bibles, our historic prayers, and in that church fabric. Let's rediscover them. Some, after all, are associated with local wells, springs, rivers, woods, and hills. Let's rethink our 'post-modern' bare as wine-bar church architecture, restore stars and angels, trees and fields, saints and animals, and living – the real thing – plants and flowers! Let us sometimes bring pets, and seeds, living soil, and field and garden produce to our services. We need more sensitivity and awareness that we're in communion with children, housebound brethren, angels and saints, flowers, stars, fire, water – all these are within our liturgical heritage, our ancient prayers, and churches. Some still remember the fenland wind blowing the day Tim and Bess Cooper were wed in Earl Soham parish church, with its biodiverse bench ends, carved by local craftsmen. The congregation filed out of church, behind Tim and Bess, singing Psalm 98, literally clapping hands with the swaying trees, and singing polyphonically with the sea birds and the winds. It was an evangelical wedding that liturgised the cosmos!

Sacred buildings, including English parish churches, chapels, majestic cathedrals, temples, even quiet rooms set aside for silence and prayers, express the same deep human instinct that sanctifies certain outdoor wells and woods and mountains. The visibility of a sacred place, like the sight of people walking to a synagogue, mosque, or church, at Sabbath, is itself a testimony, a gospel in practice. Whenever a building, set aside as 'God's house', is 'deconsecrated' and put to 'alternative use', even when worthy, we are somewhat poorer. God's houses and their living surroundings are precious places in our built environment.

Outdoor services are in continuity with indoor worship. Christians have always celebrated garden, orchard, field, wilderness, river, and sea services. We have numerous holistic hymns, including recent ones like John Rutter's *Holly Hymn*. Water blessings are popular, such as blessings of the sea and boats at Hastings, and where people pray near sacred springs, wells, rivers, lakes or seas, by annually blessing and returning the living waters, in Christ, to God. Baptismal services, and outdoor blessings of woods and waters, fields and orchards, are opportunities to remind ourselves of the presence of the cosmic Jordan, and the sacredness of the water, and virtual water, or fertile soil, entrusted to us. Ancient prayers, like that of Jacob of Sarugh, are relevant now more than ever as water and climatic disruptions, fuelled by human greed, worsen: 'The entire nature of the waters perceived that you had visited them – seas, deeps, rivers, springs and pools all thronged together to receive the blessing from your footsteps.' A lot can be done to respect this earth, where Christ walked, where he was baptised, and shed tears, blood and water onto the soil – we can include in our eucharists, in our commemoration of him, the grounds, and garden beds and plants around our churches and chapels. Even inner city chapels have a bed, or at least a container, with a living soil community, which glorifies God with us. Animal Blessings, as on the feast of St Francis or St Cuthbert, encourage children and animal-tending neighbours to pray with us, and to bring animals to church. The blessing at St John the Divine's animals' service in New York, witnesses to our shared creaturehood, our kinship, with other sensate beings:

Maker of all living creatures;
you called forth fish in the sea
birds in the air and animals on the land.
You inspired Saint Francis to call all animals
his brothers and sisters.

We ask you to bless this animal;
enable it to live according to your plan.

I lay my hands upon you in the name of the one Creator.
O Lord, we ask your blessing upon ...
In services of reconciliation, we acknowledge our failings, like
Peter in the courtyard, before our local community. When we
express contrition, and promise satisfaction, let us include cruelty
to animals, climate abuse, hurting the earth. We can always improve our earth caring, earth loving, atmosphere respecting,
cosmic Christ revering. It is good visibly to recognise the earth
as God's, to love every creature, to make that long journey from
heart to hand.

Those Special Gifts
What each of us does – how we live sustainably locally – depends, in part, on our special gifts, distinctive to each person.
Gerard Manley Hopkins writes of this distinctiveness, in Christ,
of each of us:

Christ – for Christ plays in ten thousand places,
Lovely in limbs, and lovely in eyes not his
To the Father through the features of men's faces.
(As kingfishers catch fire)

Each of us lacks gifts too. I'm not at all technically gifted, but
rather a technology no-go area. I can open a bottle of organic
wine, often with Barbara watching the bottle anxiously, and
even coming to the rescue. Left to my own devices, I would still
use a reliable hand mower to cut grass, which seems shamelessly
Mennonite and mad to post-modern gardeners, who are themselves helpless without noisy, fossil fuel guzzling machinery.
And I still prefer to think, and write, in person rather than
through a processor.

It took Barbara and me a few years to discover our gifts, defi-
ciencies, and opportunities, where we could best assist in healing, and serving, the earth community. We seriously considered
a few decades back, taking over a rundown small-holding in the
Lincolnshire wolds, so we could restore a part of the earth, in

partial self-sufficiency. But Ignatian discernment, first imbibed back in the novitiate, guided me to ecological theology, where I could assist the Christian green movement with my theological training, and to organic food growing, which correlates with and, for me at least, is inherent in ecological theology. These convictions were confirmed that day at the Fountains Abbey grange. So instead of regenerating, planting, and getting to know intimately a part of the windy wolds, I struggle with ecological theology, writing and lecturing in and near my organic fruit and vegetables, regenerating a part of overdeveloped outer suburbia. Barbara discerned along with me, following her own good angels. Instead of working the small-holding, with some animals, she's in the garden here with me, kilnering and preserving at harvest, and active in several church and environment groups.

Our theology evenings still go strong and ecumenically, some twenty of us meeting quarterly, in our lounge, overlooking the garden, accompanied by Bertha's snores, and, in winter, a log fire. Most evenings we discuss an article from a journal, a lecture, or a chapter from a book. We also utilise local expertise, some of it from within our own group. Michael Campling, for example, guided us through evenings on George Herbert, and on Mother Julian of Norwich, in both of whom he has an interest and expertise. Peter King led a discussion on Teilhard de Chardin. Keith Innes, who did special studies on the Bible and wilderness, led a discussion on wilderness. Tony Graham, of Sabeel, joined us to explain Sabeel's work, and showed how nationalist Zionists misuse the Bible. Michael Brydon, who did doctoral studies on Richard Hooker, presented an evening on that interesting thinker. Christopher Campling came from Worthing to discuss with us music and faith. We also host January Academic Inns, with a similar format to those in London and Swindon, except that the 'Inn', again, is our lounge, the meal a buffet provided by amateur, local caterers. Bexhill Academic Inn speakers have included the Revs Neil Chatfield, Con Foley, and Elizabeth Cresswell, Councillor Matthew

Wilson, and Rother District Council Sustainability Officer, Scott Lavocah. Academic Inns, especially in a Christian community, are one way of continuing Jesus' commensal ministry and symbolising effectively the beginning of the shared kingdom. We average about thirty-two persons. We also host occasional sherry evenings for groups from our churches, usually about fifteen people of varied ages and backgrounds, who regularly worship together, and appreciate the opportunity to share conversation and the fruit of the vine together. We try to offer dinner hospitality about once a month, featuring Barbara's organic and free-range cuisine, and local wines. The dinners are especially appreciated at harvest. But even on dark nights the meals include leeks, kale, sprouts, chard, leaf beet and potatoes, supplemented by kilners and preserves from summer. Winter too is at least virtual harvest.

Organic Kestrels and French Crab
I noted that theology, certainly ecological theology, includes organic gardening – and its many hands-on equivalents. These equivalents include assisting children's wildlife and gardening groups, digging and managing ponds or other wildlife habitats, cultivating beds near chapels, sharing compost, supporting local conservationists, planting trees, caring for part of an urban park, and tending window boxes and bird feeders. Getting publicly involved includes ornithology surveys, campaigns, green politics, supporting NGOs, the UNA, UNED, Eco-Schools clubs, local authority officers with responsibility for the environment – the list is as endless as are the needs. I have said a lot about organic growing. There are other needs too. I know a priest who, each year, from seeds to seedlings, plants one hundred deciduous trees, helping the Woodland Trust reforest parts of this deforested island. I also know teenagers who have managed school ponds and wildlife areas, and I know an elderly woman who contributes from her meagre savings to help younger conservationists. From her small room to which she is almost confined, she feeds small birds, making her window ledge a micro-conserv-

ation area. All of us, sooner or later, are window ledge conservationists. From that important perspective, we can reflect on,
perhaps write, ecological theology – and, above all, encourage
supple, younger conservationists.

My own habitat, including our home with its window ledges
and northerly wall, approximates about one-third of an acre.
The eighty-five fruit trees and bushes I have planted include a
worcesterberry cutting from the famous, and now vanished,
Rivers of Sawbridgeworth nursery, and a White Grape white-
currant from Roger of Pickering. These are now mainly mature,
bird swarming, fruitful in season, especially beautiful in the
growing season and harvest – but beautiful and fascinating all
year including winter. Once started, fruit growing is largely nurture, protection from parasites, pruning, tying in, healing, encouraging, harvesting – comparable with nurturing a child, an
animal, a habitat. Occasionally one of the leafy family needs re-
moval – and is missed, like a deceased animal. Our delicious Fall
Gold raspberries, which ripen in autumn, almost fool the blackbirds, but became too rampant for a suburban garden. They in-
filtrated our friendly neighbour's garden, and rampaged all
over our own border, or 'kitchen garden', where Barbara likes to
step out in all seasons for some parsley, land cress, radishes,
spring onions and, in summer, a lettuce, courgette, tomato, or
pepper. So regretfully, I uprooted those rambunctious expatri-
ates, replacing them with indigenous Malling Jewel raspberries
that are less hyperactive than Fall Gold and Autumn Bliss.
Another casualty was in the small crescent of soil, north-facing
and against the wall, which I had chiselled out of concrete
('ground forcing' in reverse), letting life and rain through again,
and where I planted a Japanese wineberry. Unfortunately, the
Channel gales, racing around the wall, battered and extinguished the wineberry, and then a Chester and an Adrienne
blackberry which I planted as replacements. Finally I planted a
sucker from my boisterous boysenberry (a cross between a
youngberry and loganberry) which has settled in, winning life's
battles, and giving fruit in the teeth of the gales. Whenever peo-

ple, in town or country – and I hope they are increasing – restore
life, where previously there had been unnecessarily the black
death of asphalt, cement, and now coloured tiles, they reverse
the 'ground forcing', really earth abuse, of some television 'gardeners' and their earth illiterate disciples. This poem well captures our modern pathology:

Uproot those trees
(Where the blackbirds nest),
Wrench out that bush
(That the bees like best),
Take up that lawn of peaceful green,
It's where we want a car to be.
Bring in pebbles, sand, cement,
Paving, bricks and mortar.
We've bought a lovely motor-car
for our seventeen-year-old daughter.
And once the concrete's all been done,
We'll plant a Peugeot for our son.
(Eileen M. C. Gray)

Despite our fruit 'full house', we still seem to add new members
to the family occasionally. I just mentioned that boysenberry
sucker. I also recently introduced four slender 'ballerinas', upright, branchless trees which take little space and need little
pruning: a Waltz, a Charlotte, a Maypole crab, and at the edge of
the wildlife area, near St Francis of Assisi, a cherry plum. I also
planted a blueberry there, beneath a neighbour's many wintered
oak, and a cranberry near my thornless loganberry. I squeezed a
Shropshire damson next to my Kentish Farleigh to help filter
east winds. On a north-facing fence I found space for a
Tummelberry, and a Waldo blackberry. An Oregon Thornless
blackberry replaced the withered Parsley Leaf blackberry in the
shade near the compost bins, where the Parsley Leaf was termin-
ally unhappy. I'm definitely out of space now, restricted to occasional replacements. We shall see. One gets attached to fruit,
similar to attachment to much loved animals. We gradually
learn the special characteristics – and special gifts! – of our fruit,

their whims, needs, foibles, and vulnerability. In July the garden literally bursts with soft fruit. From August the top fruit falls from branches, distantly similar to some of those Victorian descriptions of the Tien Shan range in Kazakhstan before deforestation and 'improvement'. We find ourselves using affectionate names for our fruit. The D'Arcy Spice, for example, an Essex man, we call 'D'Arcy'; Josephine de Malines is Josephine; while Tom Putt and Sam Young, shoulder to shoulder on the west house wall, are Tom and Sam. I sometimes wonder about the persons, women especially, for whom fruit was named. I was tempted to plant a Millicent Barnes apple, like Josephine de Malines, because of that mellifluous, intriguing name, and a Helen blackberry, because my mother's name was Helen. Space prohibits. But I would have liked to know them. Moving house, to which often I have been fated, means leaving one's fruit, for which one has laboured, and which has shared beauty, food, and fragrance in return. Leaving companionable fruit, like leaving much appreciated neighbours, is the hardest thing about moving.

Beyond the parameters of a garden, there is usually, in the neighbourhood, space requiring some 'green guerrillaism'. We removed a dead Rowan on a nearby verge and replaced it with another, which we have watered, manured, and tended. We added to our own bare verge an Amelanchier, or Juneberry, and to a bare green space around the corner a bush cherry. With absentee, sub-contractor gardeners, who visit their charges only occasionally, ailing or dead trees get little attention or replacement. As soon as we spot a vandalised tree, we prune it as best we can, and paint the wounds. Attacking other living beings, like nest robbing, is symptomatic of repressed rage at being little loved, even abused as a child, and frequently not even knowing one's father. In a psychologically damaged community, which ours certainly is, all living beings suffer. For all are connected. It's best to repair wounded trees as soon as noticed, lest the torn branches attract further assaults from wounded young men.

Like pekes, trees and bushes don't demand a great deal of

love, but they do need a steady supply. Reputable climatologists warn that before this fateful century ends, people may be unable to grow apples in southern England. The poem just quoted, and expanded food miles and air travel, show why. Motor emissions are a prime climate damager. Apple trees need cold winters, with some snappy nights. Already I notice earlier blossoming, measurable almost by the year. We used to return from March visits to John Seymour's Wexford, and Wales, to find our cherry plum in first glory on St Patrick's Day. Now it blossoms in February, as do two in my neighbour's hedge, when few insects are stirring. Hand pollination is no more a substitute for nature's biodiverse symbiosis than are genetically modified (or mutilated!) plants an improvement on natural selection, and good husbandry. I harvest fewer cherry plums than I did some years ago. The worry is that this harbinger will spread to other plums, pears and apples, and the whole family. Meanwhile, I'll plant more fruit when vacancies occur, and support alternative energies, and climate friendly transport. My four upright cordon pears on the east-facing front wall, with the compact Seckel I squeezed into the lawn, and Josephine de Malines, Gorham, and Red Williams in the back, blossom and fruit well in most springs, despite the shortage of insects. The front cordons, when in blossom or in fruit, dazzle tradesmen and passers-by.

The one tree that resists fruiting is Alfred, the apricot, despite its sheltered south-facing fence. I suspect it's because the early delicate mauve blossoms emerge when the few insects around are still dozy from winter and avoid south-west winds. Unlike the sheltered Alfred, I put our Victoria plum in almost full shade, near the compost, because Victoria is good natured and adaptable. The human Victorians used to plant some Victorias on north-facing walls to prolong the plum season when plums on warmer walls were finishing. Victoria obliged. Mine too fruits well in the shade, as its predecessor did in Ripon. A much more delicate, less adaptable plum than Victoria, our Coe's Golden Drop, a native of Bury St Edmunds, began cropping lightly after four years settling in. An annual twelve or fifteen

Coes, shaped and tasting like dripping golden drops, fill human mouths flush with sweetness, like Hopkins' 'lush capped, plush capped sloe'. I try to 'tithe', or share, some Coes, gages, and soft fruit with local clergy, and with flat dwellers and others forced to buy chemical Victorias, greengages, or tough imported Santa Rosa plums, all of which taste like wet tennis balls. Probably my best all-rounder plum is Early Transparent Gage, which nurserymen give rave reviews, saying, 'If I could only plant one plum or gage ...' So I planted two, one in the centre of the garden, the only fruit so favoured, and another against the fence, beneath those leylandii. The nurserymen were right. Although a relatively light cropper, Early Transparent is compact for a plum, with delicious fruits, suitable for small gardens. The only other fruit of which I have more than one are rhubarb, strawberries, and raspberries, three boysenberries, and two tayberries. Anything from under a leylandii is a bonus. We get a few gages most years from the Early Transparent Gage, and a few boysenberries and tayberries from beneath those ground sterilising imported leylandii.

We are entrusted with the earth, its animals, and soil fertility, on behalf of the future. Experimentation with food growing – and preserving – is one way of sharing with the future. Late keeper apples and pears can contribute to sustainable food production, they can be stored in a cellar, shed, cool room, or garage. They contribute to local sufficiency, and use no energy for transport or storage. My dwarf Bramley, our only remnant from the garden that preceded ours, gives a bumper crop biennially, and even in sabbatical years gifts us with a few. In very cool storage Bramleys keep until Easter. English cookers gradually lose the valuable acidity that make them such good cookers, so gardeners should enjoy them from soon after harvest. With climate change my other keepers, Ecklinville, Crawley Beauty, D'Arcy Spice, Leathercoat Russet, and Forge, don't keep well after Candlemass. So I planted a French Crab (really a large cooker/cordon), reputedly the latest keeper in the kingdom, on a west-facing house wall. It lives up to expectations, again biennially. Some French Crabs remain on the tree until mid-April, when other cordons are blossoming for another season. They are a good, sweet cooker. Late keepers, with various preserved fruit, fill the food gap, when little local food is around. 'Mind the gap' is a wise adage for anyone trying to live sustainably locally, especially on islands, and during climate change. Fossil fuel dependent islands, such as Britain, Ireland, and Malta, are more vulnerable to shortages, even possible hunger, than countries with contiguous borders, especially during the gap between Lent and July. John Fowler and Christopher Jones, of Farm Crisis Network, visited the garden during the gap, surveying our late sprouts, kale, chard, and broccoli. John remarked that in Africa they call the space between seasons 'the hunger gap'. The more we can shorten our gap, and fill with local food the weeks between Holy Week and Wimbledon fortnight, the better for ourselves, the climate, farmers and growers, Africa and Asia, and our children's future. During that gap we harvest early rhubarb, mostly Timperley, and Hammonds Early, and go quickly through what remains of Barbara's preserves. Kilnered, or frozen, boysenberries, blackberries, youngberries, and tayberries, mixed with rhubarb and yoghurt, are not bad fare, while awaiting the English strawberries, associated with Wimbledon. We still have to buy some local, artificially stored Cox and Bramleys. England and Ireland, and other 'trade' addicted countries, should replant their uprooted orchards promptly. England has torn out 60 per cent of its orchards in the past forty years. As a result of such hubris, and wanton folly, Britain could now be only 5 per cent self sufficient in fruit. The gap is an annual lesson – it shows the hubritic fragility of import dependence, and the 'partial' lurking in 'self-sufficiency'.

Apple Seeds
One way to preach hope is to be 'fruit tree people'. Nearly everywhere in a neighbourhood, beginning with homes, schools, and churches, there is space for small trees and bushes. Fruit plants make a precious gift for all seasons and occasions, whether pur-

chased from a nursery, or propagated from a favourite plant. It's easy to root soft fruit cuttings – in one season you have a new living being, a fruit giving life! It's even easier to dig, and re-plant, 'suckers' lifted from around favourite berries. Sharing fruit proliferates life, a wonderful way to 'edenise' your locality – at scant cost, save a few minutes of your time. Sometimes you can plant your gift at a site your recipient designates, especially if she or he is learning fruit basics. Sometimes the rooted cut-tings, or suckers, produce progeny of their own – and you're a giver of a hundredfold. Those clever with their hands can learn how to graft fruit, and propagate and share, rare and succulent fruit by grafting. Fruit trees and bushes provide companionship, beauty, shade, fragrance, food, atmosphere, and a habitat for wildlife; they symbolise the future kingdom (Rev 22:2). A red, white, or pink currant, a cherry plum, a crab apple, or damson makes a home, chapel, church, or school like a temple, wildlife welcoming, a heaven haven. Our own fruit, planted and tended and loved, with our assistance, liturgises the cosmos outdoors. In a small way it helps us to be 'monks and nuns in the temple of the earth'. I think we should celebrate fruit tree eucharists, preferably in the dormant season, because that's when we plant bare root trees, and when people especially seek signs of hope. We can model our fruit tree eucharists on the tree planting eu-charists of some southern African free churches. The tree is planted before the eucharist, by a deacon or lay minister, and nurtured thereafter by selected volunteers from the eucharist community.[9] Everywhere communicants can inform organisers of services, whenever we have planted a tree in our own garden, or school, or hospital grounds. The tree will then be included in our services; with us it offers praise, thanksgiving, and glory to God. Every tree symbolises the cross, and is related to the tree that became the cross. Joseph Plunkett's beautiful and famous poem is ecologically true: 'His cross is every tree.' Growing fruit organically, near homes, churches, and chapels, provides a rest-ing place for composted flowers, grass cuttings, kitchen rem-nants, even organic litter picked up while walking. Shakespeare's

Lear said the art of our necessities is strange that makes vile things precious. There are no vile things, only vile deeds with things. Compost, like manure, is precious, life giving, symbolic of final transformation. Every church deserves its compost corner.

Salvation Ecology Tomorrow

As John Henry Newman said, 'By the force of the incarnation, we are taught that matter is an essential part of us, and, as well as mind, is capable of sanctification.'[10] The earth community, renewed and transformed, shares our future. All material creation will be transformed into a worshipping community. Jesus of Nazareth, God incarnate, was not technically an ecologist. Yet he observed the green fields he worked and planted, he watched the birds sing and praise, and little seeds become vegetables. He shared, and hosted, communal meals, of real bread and wine, fish, herbs and fruit, nuts and vegetables. This whole earth community, where his blood and tears remain, is saved, healed, and reconciled, with us, material as well as spiritual beings, who are his creatures.

At Hastings, where he studied theology, Pierre Teilhard de Chardin detected a missing emphasis, only now seriously being addressed, in modern theology and spirituality. Teilhard underlined the cosmic hymns in his Bible, at a time when the New Testament was used in theology largely as a quarry for proof texts for theological theses. Teilhard suggested that we include another, a cosmic, nature in Jesus. The Second Vatican Council (1962-65), where Newman and Teilhard were called 'missing fathers' because of their posthumous influence, did not refer to a third nature in Christ, but in a remarkable sentence the Council did echo Teilhard: 'By his incarnation the Son of God united himself in some sense with every human being' (*Gaudium et Spes*, 22).[11] Yves Congar OP, perhaps the leading theologian at the Council, remarked, 'Our theology of catholicity (mine in any case) is certainly too timid, insufficiently cosmic. The Pauline theology of Christ in his cosmic role and that of the pleroma permit and require one to go further.'[12] Later Pope John Paul II, who as Bishop Karl Woytyla of Cracow, had worked with Teilhard's colleague Henri de Lubac on *Gaudium et Spes*, said in his first encyclical:

> The incarnation of God the Son signifies the taking up into the unity with God not only of human nature, but in this human nature, in a sense, of everything that is 'flesh': the whole of humanity, the entire visible and material world. The incarnation, then, also has a cosmic significance, a cosmic dimension. The 'first born of all creation' becoming incarnate in the individual humanity of Christ, unites himself in some way with the entire reality of man, which is also 'flesh' ... and in this reality with all 'flesh', with the whole of creation (*Dom. et Viv.* 50.3).

We need to reinhabit the cosmic generosity of Paul, who grasped and proclaimed the cosmic fullness of Jesus risen. If we live sustainably on the earth because it is filled with Christ, more people will say, with Alastair McIntosh, 'If that's what Christianity's about, then I'm all for it.' As the Risen Jesus of the Marcan appendix tells us, our mission is to preach the gospel to the whole creation.

'A New Type of Thinking'
After the atomic bomb's invention, and its use in Japan against his advice, Albert Einstein said humanity now indwells a new habitat, to which we will adapt or perish. The old techniques and paradigms, the more of the same, that failed to prevent war in the pre-bomb era, and fail to bring peace under neo-conservatives now, will not do. Einstein knew that other states, even individuals, eventually would possess the bomb. 'A new type of thinking is essential, if mankind is to move to higher levels,' he said. 'We have no lasting secret.'

No lasting secret. The principal architect of the bomb, physicist Robert Oppenheimer said, 'In some crude sense which no vulgarity, no humour, no overstatement can quite extinguish, the physicists have known sin; and this is knowledge they cannot lose.' Oppenheimer, who died a pacifist, said an individual could smuggle a bomb into New York in a suitcase, obliterate a megalopolis, and irradiate the living and non-living inhabitants of North America. Oppenheimer and Einstein have been proven right. We have no lasting secret. After Chernobyl erupted, I could call my garden in North Yorkshire pesticide, chemical, and GM free, but no longer radiation free. A new way of thinking, and reconciling, is essential, very new and different from any simplistic 'war against terrorism'.

What Einstein and Oppenheimer said about the bomb, its availability, and the need for a new way of thinking is equally true of the massive, and lethal, power of technologies in our age. We can mine the oceans, fire the forests, pierce the ozone, poison fresh water, walk on and litter other planets, manipulate cells of plant and animal life, and alter the climate. A radically reverent 'new way of thinking', and acting – more humble and loving towards the earth – is essential 'if mankind is to move to higher levels', indeed if we are to survive. As the two wise Patriarchs, of East and West, said together in Venice in 2002, it's a long way from the head to the heart, longer still from heart to hand. The few timid, querulous, and almost irrelevant international gatherings, or 'earth summits', to implement 'sustainable development', have never even come close to the 'new way of thinking', and behaving, which is necessary if people, and our planetary ecosystems dominated by people, are to survive. Politicians, corporations, and the mass media, like globalised Marshall planners, unable to think, let alone live, within parameters of restraint, reverence, humility, and love of the earth, almost autistic in their disability to relate to the earth, still cling to threadbare myths of 'economic growth', 'development', and 'progress'. We have become a globalised species, with vast, even nuclear, technologies, more earth illiterate than our ancestors, prone to hate, shoot, stab, pollute and bomb each other.

We need a new way of relating to the earth as filled with the fullness of Christ, not as 'resources' to dominate for 'economic growth', 'development', and now 'free trade' for the 'market economy', but an earth of interdependent creatures, relational beings, all filled with the fullness, the pleroma, of Christ. As Ignatius Loyola wrote to Frances Borgia in the sixteenth century, 'The fullness of our eternal God dwells in all created things, giving them being and keeping them in existence with his infinite being and presence.'[13] In commitment to 'our eternal God', to Jesus Christ, Lord and Saviour, present in all created things, we can heal and let be the earth. Because we are Jesus people, we can nurture the earth community as created sisters and brothers. If, as Barbara Ward said, we listen to the wise people and prophets among us, we may yet avoid the extinction of which they warn. None of us alone, not even all who read this book, can change all that needs changing, or heal all that needs healing. But by responding to Jesus, dwelling in the earth, by making the journey from head to heart to hand, by living sustainably locally, by loving the created earth community, and liturgising the cosmos, we can make a difference. We can be part of the solution. We can plant fruit trees. We can heal that part of earth entrusted to us. We can leave our local earth community a little better than we found it. We can let God's glory through, God's glory shining in the face of Jesus Christ.

Notes:
1. *The Erich Fromm Reader*, R. Funk, ed. (New Jersey: Humanities Press, 1994), pp. 51-52.
2. Alex Wright, *Why Bother with Theology?* (London: Darton, Longman & Todd, 2002), p. 31.
3. Alastair McIntosh, *Soil and Soul, People Versus Corporate Power* (London: Aurum Press, 2001), p. 234.
4. Sustain, *The Jellied Eel, London Food Link's Newsletter*, 1 (Summer 2002), p. 1.
5. Peter Brears, Maggie Black, Gill Corbishley, Jane Renfrew, and Jennifer Stead, *A Taste of History, 10,000 Years of Food in Britain* (London: The British Museum Press, 1997), p. 71.
6. Harvey Cox, 'Living in the New Dispensation', *The Atlantic Monthly* (March 1999), pp. 18-23.

7. John Paul II, *The Ecological Crisis: A Common Responsibility*, 16 (Washington DC, United States Conference of Catholic Bishops, 1990); cf. United States Conference of Catholic Bishops, *Global Climate Change: A Plea for Dialogue, Prudence, and the Common Good* (Washington: 2001).

8. Dulles, *Catholicity of the Church*, p. 36.

9. Edward P. Echlin, 'An African Church sets the example', *The Ecologist*, Vol. 30, 1 (January/February 2000), p. 43.

10. Newman, *Essay on Development*, p. 326.

11. *Decrees of the Ecumenical Councils, 2 Vols., Vol. 2, Trent-Vatican II*, Norman Tanner SJ, ed. (Georgetown: Sheed & Ward, 1990), p. 1082.

12. Dulles, *Catholicity of the Church*, p. 38.

13. 'Epistolae et Instructiones S Ignatii', 12 vols, *MHSJ*, Vol. 12 (Madrid: 1903, 1911), p. 667.

Some Useful Resources

Agricultural Christian Fellowship, Manor Farm, West Haddon, Northampton NN6 7AQ.

ASWA (Anglican Society for the Welfare of Animals), PO Box 7193, Hook RG27 8GT.

Audobon Society, 700 Broadway, New York, NY 10003, USA.

Brogdale Horticultural Trust, Brogdale Road, Faversham, Kent ME1 8XZ.

CCA (Catholic Concern for Animals), Laburnam Cottage, East Hanney, Oxon OX12 0JF.

Centre Naturopa, Environment, Conservation and Management Division, Council of Europe, f-67075 Strasbourg Cedex.

Christian Ecology Link, 3 Bond Street, Lancaster LA1 3ER.

Christian Socialist Movement, Westminster Central Hall, London SW1H 9NH.

Church and Conservation Project, Arthur Rank Centre, Stoneleigh, Warwickshire CV8 2LZ.

Compassion in World Farming, 5A Charles Street, Petersfield, Hampshire GU32 3EH.

CPRE (Campaign to Protect Rural England), 128 Southwark Street, London SE1 0SW.

CRUC (Christian Rural Concern), 5 Cedar Court, Addington Road, Sanderstead, South Croydon CR2 8RA.

Earthwatch International, 3 Clock Tower Place, Suite 100, Box 75, Maynard, MA 01754, USA. *Earthwatch Europe*, 267 Banbury Road, Oxford OX2 7HT.

EcoCongregation, Arthur Rank Centre, Stoneleigh, Warwickshire CV82LZ.

EIN (Environmental Issues Network of Churches Together in Britain and Ireland) Bastille Court, 2 Paris Gardens, London SE1 8ND.

ETA (Environmental Transport Association), 68 High Street, Weybridge, Surrey KT13 8RS.

European Christian Environmental Network, c/o Conference of European Churches, rue Joseph II 174, B 1000 Brussels.

Farm Crisis Network, Manor Farm, West Haddon, Northampton NN6 7AQ.

Forum for the Future, 9 Imperial Square, Cheltenham, Gloucestershire GL50 1QB.

Friends of the Earth, 26/28 Underwood Street, London N1 7JQ.

Friends of the Royal Botanic Gardens, Kew, Richmond, Surrey TW9 3AB.

Fruit Nurseries:
Deacons Nursery, Godshill, Isle of Wight PO38 3HW.
F.V. Roger, The Nursery, Pickering, North Yorkshire YO18 7HG.
Scotts Nursery, Merriott, Somerset TA16 5PL.
Walcot Organic Nursery, Lower Walcot Farm, Walcot Lane, Drakes Broughton, Pershore WR10 2AL.

Green Democrats, 144 Radford Road, Leamington Spa, Warwickshire CV31 1LQ.

Green Party (England and Wales), 1a Waterlow Road, London N19 5NJ.

Green Party (Ireland), 5a Upper Fownes Street, Dublin 2.

Green Party (Scotland), PO Box 14080, Edinburgh EH10 6YG.

Greenpeace, Canonbury Villas, London N1 2PN.

HDRA (Henry Doubleday Research Association), Ryton Organic Gardens, Coventry CV8 3LG.

ICOREC (The International Consultancy On Religion, Education and Culture), 3 Wynnstay Grove, Fallowfield, Manchester M14 6XG.

Irish Seed Savers, Capparoe, Scariff, Co. Clare.

Irish Wildlife Trust, Garden Level, 21 Northumberland Road, Dublin 4.

ISEC-UK (International Society for Ecology and Culture), Foxhole, Dartington, Devon TQ9 6EB. *ISEC-USA,* PO Box 9475, Berkeley, CA 94709.

John Muir Trust, 41 Commercial Street, Leith, Edinburgh EH6 6JD.

John Ray Initiative, QW212, Francis Close Hall, University of Gloucestershire, Swindon Road, Cheltenham GL50 4AZ.

Lifestyle, 78 Filton Grove, Horfield, Bristol BS7 0AL.

Mothers' Union, Mary Sumner House, 24 Tufton Street, London SW1P 3RB.

National Wildlife Federation, 11100 Wildlife Center Drive, Reston, VA 20190-5362.

National Resources Defense Council, 40 West 20th Street, New York, NY 10011.

Nature Conservancy, Worldwide Office, 4245 North Fairfax Drive, Suite 100, Arlington, VA 22203-1606.

Network of Christian Peace Organizations, 21 Cuckoo Hill Road, Pinner, Hertfordshire HA5 1AS.

Newfields Organics, The Green, Fadmoor, North Yorkshire.

Noah Project, Jewish Education, Celebration and Action for the Earth, PO Box 1828, London W10 5RT.

Pax Christi, Christian Peace Education Centre, St Joseph's Watford Way, Hendon, London NW4 4TY.

RSNC (Royal Society for Nature Conservation), The Kiln, Waterside, Mather Road, Newark, Nottinghamshire NG24 1WT.

SERA (The Socialist Environment and Resources Association), 11 Goodwin Street, London N4 3HQ.

Scottish Natural Heritage, 12 Hope Terrace, Edinburgh EH9 2AS.

Sierra Club, National Headquarters, 85 Second Street, 2nd Floor, San Francisco, CA 94105.

Society, Religion and Technology Project, 45 High Street, Edinburgh EH1 1SR.

Soil Association, Bristol House, 40-56 Victoria Street, Bristol, Avon BS1 6BY.

Spiritearth, 1515 W. Ogden Avenue, La Grange Park, IL 60526-1721.

Traidcraft, Kingsway, Gateshead, Tyne & Wear NE11 0NE.

Transport 2000, The Impact Centre, 12-18 Hoxton Street, London N1 6NG.

UNA (United Nations Association), 3 Whitehall Court, London SW1A 2EL.

Union of Concerned Scientists, National Headquarters, 2 Brattle Square, Cambridge, MA 02238-9105.

VOICE of Irish Concern for the Environment, 7 Upper Camden Street, Dublin 2.

Wells for India, The Winchester Centre, 68 St George's Street, Winchester SO23 8AH.

WEN (Womens Environmental Network), PO Box 30626, London E1 1TZ.

Womens Institute, National Federation of Womens Institutes, 104 New Kings Road, London SW6 4LY.

Select Bibliography

Agnew, Una, *The Mystical Imagination of Patrick Kavanagh, A Buttonhole in Heaven* (Dublin: The Columba Press, 1998).

Atherton, Mark, ed., *Celts and Christians* (Cardiff: University of Wales Press, 2002).

Baker, S., Kousis, M., Richardson, D. and Young, S., eds., *The Politics of Sustainable Development* (London: Routledge, 1997).

Barbour, Ian, *When Science Meets Religion* (London: SPCK, 2000).

Barr, James, *Biblical Faith and Natural Theology* (Oxford: Clarendon Press, 1993).

Bastaire, Helene et Jean, *Lettre de François D'Assise sur la Fraternitè Cosmique* (Paris: Parole et Silence, 2001).

Bauckham, Richard and Hart, Trevor, *Hope Against Hope: Christian Eschatology in Contemporary Context* (London: Darton, Longman and Todd, 1999).

Berry, Thomas CP with Clarke, Thomas SJ, *Befriending the Earth, A Theology of Reconciliation between Humans and the Earth* (Mystic. Twenty-third Publications, 1991).

Bockmuehl, Markus, *The Cambridge Companion to Jesus* (Cambridge: CUP, 2001).

Brock, Sebastian, *The Luminous Eye* (Kalamazoo: Cistercian Publications, 1992).

Brown, Lester, *Eco-Economy, Building an Economy for the Earth* (London: Earthscan Publications, 2001).

Clark, Stephen R.L., *Biology and Christian Ethics* (Cambridge: CUP, 2000).

Conford, Philip, *The Origins of the Organic Movement* (Edinburgh: Floris Books, 2001).

Conway, Ruth, *Choices at the Heart of Technology, A Christian Perspective* (Harrisburg: Trinity Press International, 2000).

Cornell, Joseph Bharat, *Sharing Nature with Children* (Watford: Exley Publications, 1995).

Daly, Gabriel, *Creation and Redemption* (Dublin: Gill and MacMillan, 1988).

Dent, Sr Ancilla, ed., *Ecology and Faith: The Writings of Pope John Paul II* (Berkhamsted: Arthur James, 1997).

Geoffrey Duncan, ed., *What a World* (London: The Granary Press, 2002).

Eaton, John, *The Circle of Creation: Animals in the Light of the Bible* (London: SCM Press, 1995).

Echlin, Edward P., *The Deacon and Creation* (London: Church Union, 1992); *Earth Spirituality, Jesus at the Centre* (New Alresford: John Hunt, 1999/2002).

Edwards, Denis, *Jesus the Wisdom of God: An Ecological Theology* (New York: Orbis, 1995); *Earth Revealing, Earth Healing*, ed. (Collegeville: Liturgical Press, 2001).

Giffard, Terry, ed., *John Muir, His Life and Letters and Other Writings* (London: Baton Wicks Publications, 1996).

Girardet, Herbert, *Creating Sustainable Cities* (Dartington: Green Books, 1999).

Goldsmith, Edward, *The Way: An Ecological World-View* (Dartington: Themis Books, 1996).

Goodall, Jane, *Beyond Innocence: An Autobiography in Letters: The Later Years* (Markham: Houghton Miffin, 2001).

Guroian, Vigen, *Inheriting Paradise, Meditations on Gardening* (London: Darton, Longman and Todd, 2001).

Grey, Mary, *The Wisdom of Fools* (London: SPCK, 1993); *Sacred Longings: Ecofeminist Theology and Globalization* (London: SCM, 2003).

Habid, Marion, ed., *St Francis of Assisi, Omnibus of Sources* (Quincy: Franciscan Press, 1991).

Hapgood, John, *The Concept of Nature* (London: Darton, Longman and Todd, 2002).

Harvey, Graham, *The Killing of the Countryside* (London: Vintage, 1998).

Haught, John F. *God Beyond Darwin: A Theology of Evolution* (Coulder: Westview, 2000); *Deeper than Darwin: The Prospect for Religion in the Age of Evolution* (Oxford: Westview Press, 2003).

Hayes, Zachary, *A Window to the Divine: A Study of Christian Creation Theology* (Quincy: Franciscan, 1997).

Herbert, Theodore, *The Yahwist's Landscape, Nature and Religion in Early Israel* (Oxford: OUP, 1996).

Houghton, John, *Global Warming: The Complete Briefing* (Cambridge: CUP, 1997).

Johnson, Elizabeth, *Truly Our Sister: A Theology of Mary in the Communion of Saints* (New York: Continuum, 2003).

Jones, James, *Jesus and the Earth* (London: SPCK, 2003).

Lane, Dermot, *Christ at the Centre* (Dublin: Veritas, 1990); *Keeping Hope Alive* (Dublin: Gill & Macmillan, 1996).

Leopold, Aldo, *A Sand County Almanac* (Oxford: OUP, 1968).

Linzey, Andrew and Regan, Tom, eds., *Animals and Christianity, A Book of Readings* (London: SPCK, 1989).

Lohfink, Norbert, *Great Themes from the Old Testament* (Edinburgh: T. & T. Clark, 1982).

Louth, Andrew, *Wilderness* (London: Darton, Longman and Todd, 2003).

Lyons, James A., *The Cosmic Christ in Origen and Teilhard de Chardin* (Oxford: OUP, 1982).

Matthews, Anne, *Wild Nights, the Nature of New York City* (London: Flamingo, 2001).

Mayne, Michael, *This Sunrise of Wonder* (London: Fount, 1995).

McDonnell, Kilian, *The Baptism of Jesus in the Jordan* (Collegeville: Liturgical Press, 1996).

McIntosh, Alastair, *Soil and Soul, People Versus Corporate Power* (London: Aurum Press, 2001).

McKibben Bill, *The Comforting Whirlwind, God, Job, and the Scale of Creation* (Grand Rapids: Eerdman, 1994).

McPartlan, Paul, *Sacrament of Salvation, An Introduction to Eucharistic Ecclesiology* (Edinburgh: T. & T. Clark, 2000).

Meier, John, *A Marginal Jew, Rethinking the Historical Jesus*, Vol. 1 (London: Doubleday, 1991); Vol. 2 (London: Doubleday, 1994).

Millstone, Erik, and Lang, Tim, *The Atlas of Food: Who Eats What, Where and Why* (London: Earthscan, 2003).

Mooney, Christopher, *Theology and Scientific Knowledge: Changing Models of God's Presence in the World* (South Bend: University of Notre Dame Press, 1997).

Moore, Norman, *The Bird of Time* (Cambridge: CUP, 1987); *Oaks, Dragonflies and People: creating a small nature reserve and relating its story to wider conservation issues* (Colchester: Harley Books, 2002).

Morgan, Joan, *The New Book of Apples: The Definitive Guide to Over 2000 Varieties* (London: Ebury Press, 2002).

Murray, Robert, *The Cosmic Covenant* (London: Sheed & Ward, 1992).

Northcott, Michael, *The Environment and Christian Ethics* (Cambridge: CUP, 1996)

O'Donoghue, Noel Dermot, *The Mountain Behind the Mountain: Aspects of the Celtic Tradition* (Edinburgh: T. & T. CLark, 1993); *The Angels Keep Their Ancient Places* (Edinburgh: T. &T. Clark, 2001).

Oelschlaeger, Max, *Caring for Creation: An Ecumenical Approach to the Environmental Crisis* (London:Yale University, 1994).

Palmer, Martin, *Faith and Conservation* (World Bank, 2003).

Rodd, Cyril S., *Glimpses of a Strange Land, Studies in Old Testament Ethics* (Edinburgh: T. & T. Clark, 2001).

Schwartz, Richard H., *Judaism and Global Survival* (New York: Lantern, 2002).

Scott, Peter, *A Political Theology of Nature,* Cambridge Studies in Christian Doctrine (Cambridge: CUP, 2003).

Scully, Matthew, *Dominion, The Power of Man, the Suffering of Animals, and the Call to Mercy* (New York: St Martin's Press, 2002).

Seymour, John, *The Complete Book of Self-Sufficiency* (London: Dorling Kindersley, 1997); *The Fat of the Land* (New Ross: Metanoia Press, 1995).

Sorrell, Roger, *St Francis of Assisi and Nature: Tradition and Innovation in Western Christian Attitudes Toward the Environment* (Oxford: OUP, 1988).

Stack, Tom, ed., *No Earthly Estate, God and Patrick Kavanagh: An Anthology* (Dublin: The Columba Press, 2002).

Stanton, Graham, *Gospel Truth? New Light on Jesus and the Gospels* (London: Harper Collins, 1995).

Suchocki, Marjorie, *The Fall to Violence: Original Sin in Relational Theology* (New York: Continuum, 1994).

Tetlow, Joseph, ed., *Ignatius Loyola, Spiritual Exercises* (New York: The Crossroad Publishing Co., 1999).

Thompson, Paul B., *The Spirit of the Soil, Agriculture and Environmental Ethics* (London: Routledge, 1995).

Ward, Barbara and Dubois, Rene, *Only One Earth* (London: Penguin, 1972).

Wessels, Cletus, *Jesus in the New Universe Story* (Maryknoll: Orbis, 2003).

Williams, Patricia A., *Doing Without Adam and Eve: Sociobiology and Original Sin* (Minneapolis: Fortress, 2001).

Wright, N. T., *The Challenge of Jesus* (London: SPCK, 2000); *The Resurrection of the Son of God* (London: SPCK, 2003).